SHIPWRECKS FROM THE EGYPTIAN

(*Above*) The view towards the foc'sle of the *Rosalie Moller* during an early morning dive.(*Previous page*) Large steering quadrant is found on the unidentified shipwreck at Sha'ab Danaba. (*Opposite*) My diving partner swims over the remains of the *Agia Varvara* which are scattered over the reef.

SHIPWRECKS FROM THE EGYPTIAN RED SEA

Ned Middleton

Illustrated by
Rico Oldfield

Ashgrove Publishing
London

First published in Great Britain by Immel Publishing Limited.

Text © 2006, 2010 Ned Middleton
Paintings © 2006, 2010 Rico Oldfield

Ned Middleton asserts his right to be identified as the author in accordance with the Copyright, Designs & Patents Act 1988.

All photographs © Ned Middleton; except where noted.

This edition published in 2010, by Ashgrove Publishing
an imprint of Hollydata Publishers Ltd
27 John Street London WC1N 2BX

ISBN 978 185398 153 1

First Paperback Edition
Book design by Brad Thompson
Printed and bound in China

(Above) A typical underwater reef scence from the Egyptian Red Sea
(Above right) Egyptian Bedouin seen on the Sinai Peninsular.

· CONTENTS ·

Foreword / page 7

Introduction / 9

FROM NA'AMA BAY – SOUTH TO HURGHADA / 13

Chapter I
Agia Varvara / 19

Chapter II
Million Hope & Hey Daroma / 23

Chapter III
Zingara / 29

Chapter IV
Thistlegorm / 33

Chapter V
Kingston / 45

Chapter VI
Dunraven / 51

Chapter VII
Ulysses / 57

Chapter VIII
Rosalie Moller / 63

Chapter IX
Kimon M / 69

Chapter X
Chrisoula K / 75

Chapter XI
Carnatic / 81

Chapter XII
Giannis D / 89

Chapter XIII
Miniya / 95

FROM HURGHADA – SOUTH TO ROCKY ISLAND / 99

Chapter XIV
Salem Express / 103

Chapter XV
Numidia / 109

Chapter XVI
Aïda / 117

Chapter XVII
Turbo / 123

Chapter XVIII
Zealot & Maidan / 129

Appendix:

Part One: Miscellaneous Minor Wrecks / 141
Part Two: Miscellaneous Ships and Names / 146
Part Three: Missing Ships in the Gulf of Suez / 155

Acknowledgments / 157

Bibliography / 160

For Beth – Who would expect a book be dedicated to her.
For Jessica – Who would very much like a book dedicated to her.
For Daniel – Who deserves a book dedicated to him.
For Ashley & Fleur – Who might never have learned that a book is dedicated to them.

Every day in my heart.

Tiran Island which marks the entrance to the Gulf of Aqaba. Tiran island is actually in Saudi Arabia – but the Straits are administered by Egypt.

· FOREWORD ·

It was many more years ago than I care to remember, when I watched a Cousteau documentary, recording a dive on a ship somewhere in the Red Sea. The images fired my imagination to an extent which has now developed into a passion for anything associated with shipwrecks. Ned Middleton and I have subsequently become friends but I realise now that my memory has played tricks on me concerning that particular wreck. Being a steam enthusiast from childhood, it was the sight of two locomotives in the dark depths of the ship, sitting there just as if in a steam shed and I will never ever forget that vision. In fact, in the sun-lit gloom of the hold of the ship were actually a number of World War II trucks and motor cycles. However, there were indeed two steam loco-motives on board but they were blasted off the deck and are now almost unrecognisable on the seabed. The ship was the *Thistlegorm*, sunk at anchor by German bombers, in the entrance to the Suez Canal.

My interest has been further fuelled by watching the classic docu-mentaries by Ballard and others, first on the discovery and subsequent dives on the *Titanic* followed by the *Bismarck* and HMS *Hood*. Now, I regard it as a great privilege to write a few words about this book, one of many, written by a man who shares with me a passion for telling shipwreck stories, and who is unequalled in his ability to translate these into a very readable style of writing. He has consequently come to be regarded as a leading shipwreck historian, and this book is a must. He has dived on countless occasions into the Egyptian Red Sea where may be found what is regarded by many as the world's most outstanding col-lection of diveable shipwrecks and has illustrated each individual ship, dating from 1869 to 1996. Unlike the wrecks in Truk Lagoon or Bikini Atoll, each of these shipwrecks has its own very individual story to tell, no more so than the *Thistlegorm* which is visited by thousands of divers every month and has consistently remained the world's most dived shipwreck for the past ten years or more.

However, this book offers so much more. With the combination of Ned's knowledge of diving and historical research, we have the out-standing artwork of Rico Oldfield. It is something to give an impres-sion of a shipwreck but this is not enough for Rico or Ned. Photographs provided in black and white by Ned gave Rico an accurate montage from which to work. In the case of the *Thistlegorm*, Ned took over a thousand photographs. The resultant painting, along with all the others by Rico, is as accurate as it possibly can be through his unri-valled skill in this highly specialised field of painting. His wreck illus-trations show to the finest detail the final resting place of all the ships concerned.

Ned's narrative skilfully brings alive tales from World War II, instances of heroism and grave tragedy. For example, the demise of the *Salem Express*, which sank only a few years ago through sheer incom-petence on the part of the captain, resulted in four hundred and sixty lives lost. Ned also points out, no doubt with feelings of contempt, how some people plunder wrecks and how this sort of practice is quite inde-fensible – especially for those wrecks which are graves. So, what is it about shipwrecks that we find so fascinating? We only have to read the text, look at these remarkable illustrations, close our eyes and let our memories and imaginations go into overdrive; thinking of all those involved when a great ship sinks to the bottom of the seabed but is still lying there, in some cases, almost complete as though she was recently launched, and realise that we are reliving history.

Thank you Ned for granting me the privilege of writing a foreword to such a memorable work which I shall always treasure.

David Shepherd

David Shepherd OBE, FRSA, FRGS

Two divers inspect the propeller of the *Zealot* at a depth of over 85m. <small>(Kimmo Hagman)</small>

· INTRODUCTION ·

From the very moment the Suez Canal was opened in November 1869, the Red Sea became an important shipping route linking Europe and the Far East. Today that route is an international highway for many thousands of freighters, tankers, passenger liners – even warships – as they make their way from the North Atlantic to the Indian Ocean and beyond. Or vice versa. This surface traffic is particularly concentrated along the narrow confines of the Gulf of Suez, an offshoot of water approximately one hundred and fifty miles long, linking the Red Sea to the Suez Canal itself. Although significantly shorter than the twelve hundred mile alternative route via South Africa, a large part of the journey is marked by unpredictable currents and shallow coral reefs. This is especially so at the interface between the Gulf itself and the open Red Sea – an area called the Straits of Gobal. Though much simplified, these are the factors which have combined to make this northern part of the Red Sea one of the most testing stretches of water in the world. Even with modern aids to navigation, vessels still continue to founder here.

Against this backdrop of natural circumstances, ideal for scuba diving in general and wreck diving in particular, the modern diver is able to enjoy the benefits of cheap air travel and access provided by live-aboard safari boats – both of which combine to make dedicated wreck diving excursions extremely popular and very affordable. This has given rise to a new breed of holidaymaker, some of whom work physically harder during their annual – or even twice-annual – break, than at other times of the year. Twenty or thirty dives during a single week's safari or perhaps twice as many from a two-week vacation are regularly achieved by those intent on extracting the maximum diving from their trip. And why not!

The final part of the overall equation is, of course, the advent of modern diving practices. Whilst the visitor to the Red Sea does not have to be a professional diver to fully appreciate the vast majority of the wrecks detailed within this book, it is a fact that divers are becoming less content with simply viewing the external features of any sunken vessel and are more intent on probing ever deeper. Divers are explorers in the true sense of the word. As such, they are going deeper and probing further than was thought possible, even just a few short years ago. Time was when divers were generally satisfied with entering a well lit bridge through wide open doorways. Today, however, the talk is of penetration and reaching those deep and unlit recesses of the engine room and beyond.

THE SHIPWRECKS – For all grades of diver, this book sets out to describe those vessels which have come to grief in the Egyptian Red Sea. These shipwrecks – both ancient and modern – are all waiting to be investigated. They include historic vessels such as the *Carnatic*, lost in 1869 with the loss of thirty-one lives; the *Dunraven*, lost in 1876 and the *Ulysses* in 1887. All represent a fascinating insight into tragic and incredible stories from another age of transport and, in the case of the *Carnatic* with its valuable cargo, another age of diving. Then there are the wartime casualties, such as the *Thistlegorm* and *Rosalie Moller* – lost within forty-eight hours of each other in 1941, and the former Soviet minesweeper lost in a more recent conflict. Finally, there is that new breed of modern shipwreck such as the *Kimon M* (lost in 1978), the *Giannis D* (1983) and the 16,000 tonne *Million Hope* (lost as recently as 1996) – to name but three.

In recent years, the north Egyptian Red Sea has become one of the world's foremost destinations for wreck divers. It is, perhaps, fair to say that the rediscovery of the *Thistlegorm* had a lot to do with the sudden interest in the area. That said, a single shipwreck – no matter how outstanding – does not make a wreck safari. It was, therefore, inevitable, that interest would quickly extend to other vessels lost in the same locality. For a short time it even seemed as though there was a determined effort to find new wrecks, whilst those that were already well known were sud-

The luxurious *My Rosetta* is capable of sustaining 14 knots in comfort and style and is typical of the better class of diving safari boat which operate in the Egyptian Red Sea.

denly being assessed in terms of their diving potential. From then on an industry simply grew.

During my research, I frequently found myself comparing Egypt's shipwrecks to other destinations around the world and I have reached the conclusion there is no comparison. Certainly, Truk Lagoon (Sorry, I can't get used to Chuuk!), Bikini Atoll, the Caribbean and even the Mediterranean all come to mind. But consider this: For all the ships lost in Truk Lagoon, there is but a single story which explains how they came to be there. Furthermore, each of those ships was being actively used in support of the Imperial Japanese Navy on the day they were sunk in 1944. In short, there are no ships in Truk Lagoon from either 1869 or 1996. The same applies to the wrecks found on Bikini Atoll, all sunk as part of an atomic bomb experiment.

When it comes to the shipwrecks found in either the Caribbean or the Mediterranean, things are very different because both ancient and modern vessels are found here and there. That said, there is no real substantial collection of shipwrecks to be found within any single country, or relatively small area, which compares to those found in the Egyptian Red Sea. There is no single country in either the Caribbean on one side of the Atlantic Ocean, or the Mediterranean on the other, which can boast a collection of shipwrecks to compete with those found in this book. Put another way, it is quite possible to visit all the major shipwrecks detailed within this book – weather permitting – during a three-week dedicated safari. By comparison, one would have to visit almost every island in the Caribbean or several countries in the Mediterranean to find anything of similar value. With so much to offer the dedicated wreck diver – in addition to a welcoming climate and warm, clear water – it is easy to understand why this incredible ships' graveyard attracts so many scuba-diving tourists back year after year, after year.

From the moment the overall project became one of producing a book, I was determined it would be the most accurate account of each of the principle shipwrecks found within the Egyptian sector of the Red Sea. I did consider extending the book to include the Sudan and other Red Sea destinations but dismissed this, largely because the project would have become far too big. As work progressed, I insisted on keeping three distinct objectives in mind at all times:

ACCURACY – My stated aim was to produce the very first guide book containing information about all known major diveable shipwrecks found within the Egyptian Red Sea. In so doing, I was determined to make every effort to unravel all the prevailing confusion with the express intention of providing details that are as accurate and as complete as is possible to achieve.

READABILITY – For me, the account of each ship's loss and her resultant transformation from sea-going vessel to dive site is one of the most fascinating aspects of the whole adventure. Once again, with the exception of the *Thistlegorm*, I was surprised to learn the story of most of these final journeys had never previously been told, and I considered it high time that they were. Let's not forget that even the *Titanic* would have passed into obscurity – as did her sister ships – were it not for the way in which she was lost!

A BOOK FOR THE DEDICATED WRECK DIVER – A shipwreck is a very specific thing. It is a man-made object found in a place were it does not belong. And that is where the fascination lies. To this end, I sought to include all those wrecks which any wreck diver would wish to visit. The wreck at Zabargad Island, unfortunately, had to be discounted because it was officially out-of-bounds. Although we could have easily visited this fairly substantial shipwreck without anyone knowing, we were not prepared to break Egyptian laws.

Put simply, this book contains the full story behind each vessel – before, during and after her actual loss. As a result, the reader also has the author's personal assurance that every major shipwreck has been correctly identified and described. That said, I would be delighted to hear from anybody who is able to add any additional information or correct any minor errors that may have occurred. I will incorporate such information into any future editions.

SOMETHING FOR THE FUTURE – As far as my own description of each wreck is concerned, I have not included a blow-by-blow account of every nut, bolt and companionway as they are today, underwater. Such a task is not only impractical but also undesirable. There remains plenty for adventurous divers to discover for themselves. If you feel the need to discover what the bridge of the *Rosalie Moller* or the engine room of the *Giannis D* are really like, then this book will set you on the road to discovering such details for yourself. In every exciting destination, there is always something that still awaits discovery and such wrecks as the *Dacca* and *Taiwan* are very exciting prospects indeed. Many unknown ships are marked on the relevant charts and there are even more that are not.

A WORD ABOUT SAFETY – It is not for me to state which diver should or should not visit any particular wreck. I have no means of comparing experience and ability with the requirements of any dive, which in any event, might be significantly changed by adverse weather conditions. My book seeks to inform the reader about Egypt's shipwrecks. It tells the complete story of those lost ships and that is all. It is for each reader to

The massive starboard side of the *Million Hope* resting alongside of the nearby reef.

seek separate advice with regard to their own diving experience and the suitability of any particular dive.

Shipwrecks are made of steel and wood; commodities which continue to deteriorate in seawater until eventually nothing is left. They are also structures which are very heavy and are, therefore, prone to collapse at any time. This is especially so for those which lie on their side, if only because they were never designed to withstand their own weight in such circumstances. Any of the shipwrecks described in this book may have become unsafe since these words were written. All divers are strongly advised to seek up-to-date advice with regard to the current condition of any vessel which they intend to visit. Be warned – shipwrecks can be dangerous places and should always be approached with great caution.

Having said all that – do enjoy.

Ned Middleton

The long beach at Na'ama Bay on the Sinai Peninsular with the jetty at bottom right.

From Na'ama Bay – south to Hurghada

A typical scene over the stern of a diving safari boat as divers prepare for their next underwater adventure.

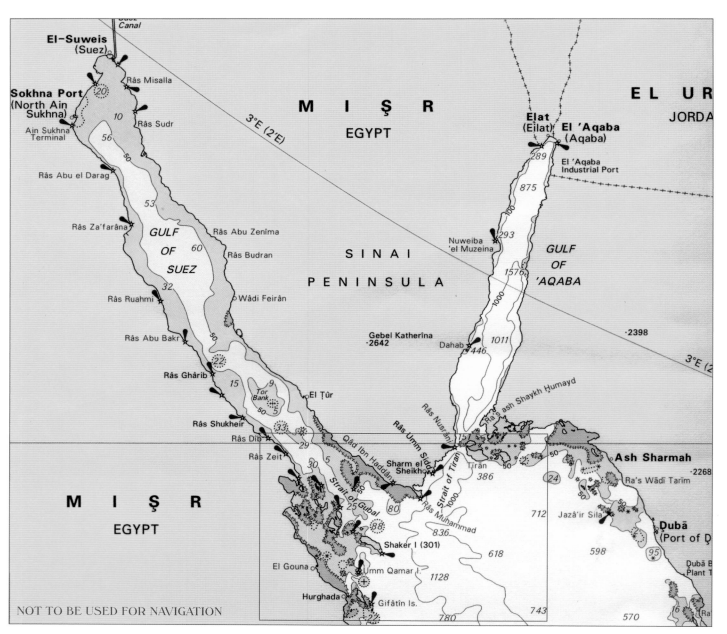

The Gulf of Suez, Sinai Peninsular, Gulf of Aqaba and northern sector of the Egyptian Red Sea as far as Hurghada.
The area boxed in red is shown opposite. (Extract from Admiralty Chart 4704, United Kingdom Hydrographic Office)

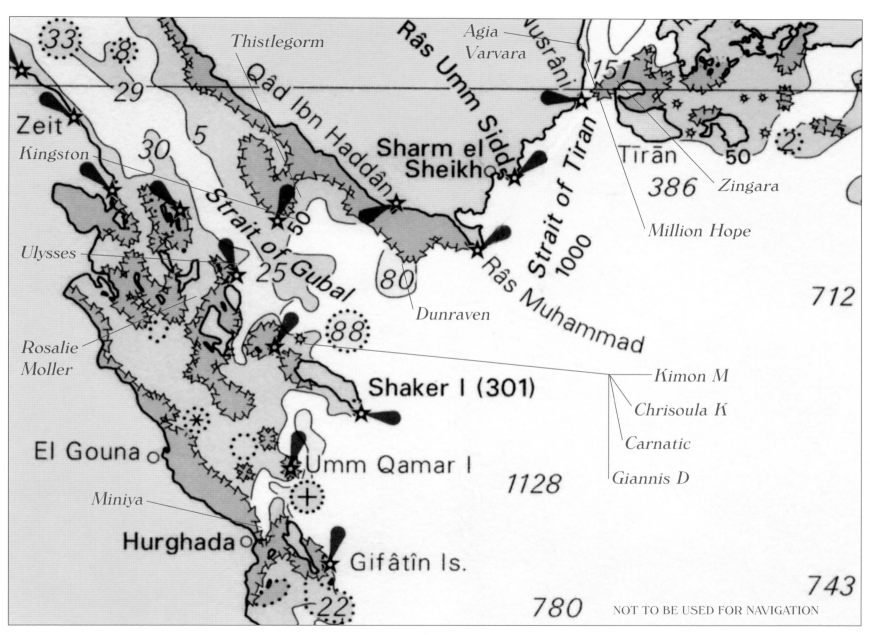

The Straits of Gobal and Straits of Tiran. Thirteen of the major shipwrecks covered by this book are found within this relatively small area.

(United Kingdom Hydrographic Office)

Some of the many species of reef fishes the diver could encounter on any dive in the Egyptian Red Sea. Clockwise from top left; Giant Moray Eel, Two-bar Anemonefish and Anemone, Orange-striped Triggerfish, Crocodilefish, Bigeye and Blue Spotted Stingray.

More reef fishes from the Egyptian Red Sea. Clockwise from top left; Shoaling Sweetlips, Grey Reef Shark, Banded Dascyllus, Blackside Hawkfish and Emperor Angelfish.

• Chapter I •

AGIA VARVARA
(GPS: 28° 03·450N, 34° 26·830E)

THE SHIP – Built by Ch & At Aug-Normand of France, the *Agia Varvara* was launched as the *Nina* in 1950. Officially described as a general cargo vessel, she was later called *Athenia*, then *Petros*, before finally becoming *Agia Varvara* in 1974. A relatively small ship for one with three cargo holds in front of a bridge and engine room located at the stern. She had a 5-cylinder oil-fired engine capable of producing 750 hp and a top speed of 10 knots. Her dimensions were 73.2m x 9.33m with a draught of 4m and a displacement of 985 gross registered tons (grt). The *Agia Varvara* was owned and operated by the Gestar Shipping Company of Famagusta, Cyprus at the time of her loss.

GETTING THE NAME RIGHT! – The word *Agia* is pronounced with a silent 'g' which has led to several wrongly spelled versions of the name. One of the leading authorities on shipwrecks includes details of this vessel's loss under the misnomer *Ayia Varvara*. Even Lloyd's List of 29 June 1976 describes this ship as the *Aghia Barbara*. My first visit to this ship was in early 2001 when confusion about the name still existed amongst local dive guides. My visit had been arranged by Scubaway, who had placed my diving in the very capable hands of Paolo Guiotto of TGI Sinai.

The *Pinta* – sister ship of the *Agia Varvara* (World Ship Society)

In my line of work I meet many dive guides. Just occasionally one sticks out from the crowd. During three weeks of fairly intensive diving, I watched Paolo in action in a variety of situations and I came to regard him as one of the very best in the business. He was also one of the most experienced in this part of the world – averaging seven hundred dives a year, for the previous seven years. Curiously, he too had never dived the *Agia Varvara* before my visit.

THE LOSS OF THE *AGIA VARVARA* – The available details of this loss are scant, to say the least. On 27 June 1976, the *Agia Varvara* sailed in ballast from the Jordanian port of Aqaba, destined for Port Said. The ship was only ninety miles further south when, in the early hours of the following morning, she drove hard onto the inshore reef near Nabq, a few miles north of Sharm El Sheikh. The crew were, subsequently, rescued by the Israeli Navy.

DIVING THE *AGIA VARVARA* – It was 08.00 hrs when we boarded the day-boat *Aziz 1* – a well-run vessel in the hands of Captain Bassem Mohammed Abu Ali. Bassem is a very competent skipper who trained as a lawyer before answering the call of the sea. A good man to have on board if ever there are any problems with over-zealous officials! We set off heading in a northerly direction and it was not long before we were passing close to the four reefs which mark the centre of the narrow interface between the Red Sea and the Gulf of Aqaba. Here the rule of the road is keep right with 'Up' traffic taking the eastern route between the reefs and Tiran Island, and 'Down' traffic keeping to the west. Jackson Reef is the most northerly of the four reefs and Gordon Reef the most southerly. Ominously, they are both marked by the prominent shipwrecks, *Lara* and *Loullia* respectively – a clear warning for all vessels entering and leaving the Gulf of Aqaba to exercise extreme care.

From some distance away we could see the superstructure of the *Million Hope* – one of the largest ships ever to have been lost in the Red Sea, and one which acts as a marker for the *Agia Varvara*. In no time at all we were passing alongside this massive ship – the keel of which rests on the seabed twenty metres below. Two hundred metres further on we saw some remnants of wreckage on the reef top. These were once the bows of the *Agia Varvara* and almost immediately we could see the rest of this vessel underwater. It was time to get wet.

A combination of a relatively shallow attitude and an exposed position mean that after twenty-five years the vessel is now rather broken up – although there are some very large parts for those who prefer bigger sections. The stern is found resting on the seabed at 20m and pointing up the reef. All the portholes are still in place and the very bent propeller is

The ship's engine block now lies exposed on the reef at a depth of about 8m.

still attached. The rudder, however, is found a short distance away. Above the stern, the diver is able to investigate inside the lower part of the bridge deck which allows access down to the engine room. Curiously, a large portion of the engines lie exposed on the reef at 6-8m.

A short distance to the north is another large section of superstructure, complete with funnel. This is the upper part of the bridge deck which became entirely separate from the remainder and now rests on the seabed at 20m. Trapped underneath is the ship's funnel, in the side of which is an open door. Large pieces of steel plating and iron cross-members litter the reef which towers over the wreckage with even more, a short distance further to the north. The foc'sle and bows appear to have remained on the surface of the reef and, over the ensuing years, have been reduced to a few remnants of scrap metal and the occasional bollard.

POSTSCRIPT – It must be said that the *Agia Varvara* is not one of Egypt's greatest shipwrecks. Had she been wrecked elsewhere, I am sure that would have been very different. Of course, she is where she is, and being largely overlooked, provides a refreshing alternative to those shipwrecks which have been systematically looted by those who think only of themselves. Interestingly, Paolo wasn't the only guide who had never dived this wreck before.

Nevertheless, the *Agia Varvara* is still a very good dive and, alongside the *Dunraven*, *Million Hope* and *Zingara*, is one of only four diveable wrecks within very easy reach of Sharm El Sheikh and could, therefore, play a more important role for those divers wishing to experience something new in this corner of the Red Sea. So, if you like virgin shipwrecks, why not be amongst the first to add the *Agia Varvara* to your diving itinerary.

My diving partner emerges from inside the stern of the *Agia Varvara*.

• Chapter II •

MILLION HOPE & HEY DAROMA

(GPS: 28° 03·400N, 54° 26·845E)

THE SHIP – Built by Koyo Dockyard Co, Mihara, Japan, as a bulk carrier with additional facilities for transporting vehicles, the *Million Hope* was launched as the *Ryusei Maru* in 1972. She measured a massive 174.6m x 24.8m with a draught of 10m and displacement of 16,774 grt. Her bridge deck is located at the stern behind five cargo holds – in between which are four massive cranes towering high above the decks. The ship was powered by two 6-cylinder diesel engines capable of producing 11,600 hp and a top speed of 17 knots.

The ship had several names during her lifetime and became the *Hope* when she was purchased by the Aksonas Shipping Company of Limassol, Cyprus. During my research, on 10 December 2003, I received an e-mail from this company stating: 'We note that you are interested in the shipwreck of the *Million Hope*. This was the ex-*Hope* which was sold by Aksonas Shipping in early February 1996 to some Chinese interests who renamed the vessel *Million Hope*. It was under the latter's ownership/

The *Million Hope* as the *Hope*. In early 1996, the *Hope* was sold and renamed *Million Hope* and it was under this latter name that she was wrecked only a short time later. Details of the ship, however, are found under the name of *Hope* in Lloyd's Register of Shipping. (FotoFlite)

management that the loss occurred.' According to Lloyd's of London, both the ship and her cargo were insured for just over four million pounds when she became a constructive total loss in June of that year.

THE LOSS OF THE *MILLION HOPE* – Loaded with a 26,000-ton cargo of potash and phosphates, the *Million Hope* sailed from Jordan's only port, Aqaba, on 19 June 1996, destination Taiwan. Visibility, however, quickly deteriorated. Early on 20 June, the vessel struck an inshore reef near Nabq – a few miles north of Sharm El Sheikh, on the eastern shores of the Sinai Peninsular.

Lloyd's List dated 24 June 1996, carried the following item:

CASUALTY REPORT:

MILLION HOPE (Cyprus) Jun 21: Egyptian Maritime Officials said yesterday they were concerned about possible leakage of about 23,000 tons of phosphate and potassium plus 700 tons of fuel from the bulk carrier *Million Hope* which sank off Egypt's Sinai Peninsula, Cairo radio reported. All twenty-five members of the crew were rescued by Egyptian naval vessels and other vessels in an operation that lasted more than twenty hours. The vessel, on voyage from Jordan to Taiwan, was ripped open by coral reefs near Egypt's Sharm El-Sheikh resort. The vessel's mainly Filipino crew huddled in the stern and refused to abandon ship until it became clear the vessel would sink, Cairo radio said. Some of the crew accused the vessel's master of failing to follow the area's prescribed navigation routes and of maintaining speed despite poor visibility.

The *Hey Daroma* as the *Lairds Loch*. When the *Million Hope* was wrecked, she came to rest on top of the hull of this ship which once served as a ferry in the Scottish Isles (Scottish Maritime Museum)

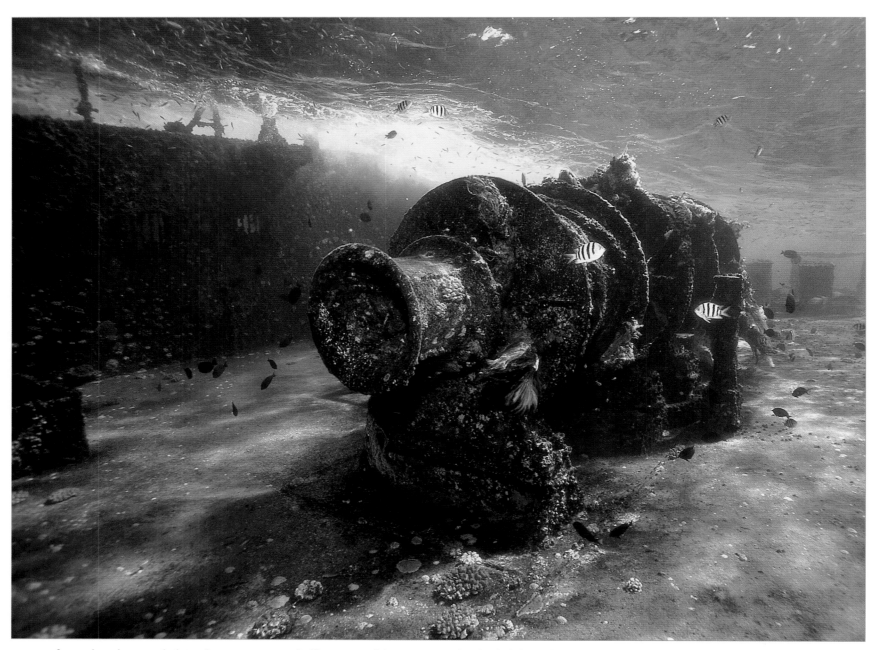

Located on the stern deck is a large mooring winch. The corner of the open access hatch which leads down to the engine room can just be seen at bottom left.

The cargo actually comprised 15,000 tons of potash and 11,000 tons of phosphate rock. The big concern was that this would slowly dissolve in seawater – producing an algae-like film that would blot out essential sunlight from all adjacent reefs. Major salvage companies were invited to tender for the salvage of the cargo, separately valued at £1·3 million. This operation was successfully carried out.

DIVING THE *MILLION HOPE* – With much of her superstructure still out of the water, the *Million Hope* can be seen from several miles away. She is basically upright, but with a pronounced list to port – i.e. away from the reef. Her entire starboard side rests close to the reef on which she foundered and her keel lies along the seabed at the base of that reef at 19-24m. Her decks are underwater, but not the foc'sle. Apart from superficial damage, the vessel is completely intact and with no evidence of salvage. All the cargo holds are entirely open, with no residue of cargo remaining.

Following the bows down to the seabed at 19m, the diver will find clear evidence of the ship's impact with the reef. Where one would normally expect to find a bulbous nose on a vessel of this size, here is the very opposite – a large dent cutting back into the ship by over a metre. On the starboard side and hidden against the reef, is further evidence of damage with bent and buckled plates stretching some distance back. If you look carefully, however, there is also evidence of another ship squashed underneath this massive vessel. This is the *Hey Daroma*.

THE *HEY DAROMA* – Built by Ardrossan Dockyards Ltd., the general cargo vessel *Hey Daroma* was launched in August 1940 as the *Lairds Loch*. She displaced 1,736 grt and had a single action 8-cylinder oil-fired engine capable of producing 2,500 hp and a top speed of 14 knots. She was 83.8m long, 12.5m wide and had a draught of 3.6m. The *Hey Daroma* was owned and operated by Sefinot Ltd. of Eilat, at the time of her loss. On the night of 3 September 1970, the *Hey Daroma* sailed from Eilat with a cargo of water and some time later struck the same inshore reef as the *Million Hope* would find almost 26 years later. All the crew were safely rescued before several attempts were made to refloat the vessel. This included one where they tried to push the wreck off the reef using large tractors. Eventually, however, the *Hey Daroma* was abandoned as a constructive total loss.

After successive winters and storms, the *Hey Daroma* eventually made her own way back to the sea and for many years was to be found in two pieces. Her bows had come to rest on the very edge of the reef-top – lying on the port side and facing south. The remainder of the hull was reported as being a little further north and upside down at the base of the reef in

My diving partner and good friend - Paolo Guiotto of TGI Sinai, inspects the massive propeller of the *Million Hope*.

18-20m of water. In 1996, however, the *Million Hope* came to rest on top of the upturned hull of the *Hey Daroma*. Today, very little of the smaller vessel is now left. Her bows are still found a few metres in front of the much larger *Million Hope* and some crushed wreckage is also found on the seabed between the *Million Hope* and the reef.

Along the port side of the *Million Hope*, the diver is able to follow the hull all the way back from bows to stern. This was a long swim and provided an excellent opportunity for me to try out my brand new Scubapro Twin Jet fins. I was fifty-years-old when I first visited this wreck and, as much as I may try and keep myself fit, I was very impressed with this new design of fin, with the split down the middle. They really did prove to be a great energy saver, well worth the additional outlay.

It may be fair to say that this part of the dive was somewhat repetitive, but we did find evidence of the ship having buckled on impact and, in places, we could see right through the damaged hull into the empty cargo holds beyond. We also came across the gantry from the No. 4 Crane, which had fallen to the seabed and was resting against the hull. At the stern, a huge propeller is found at 24m with the ends of each of its four blades bent hard over – indicating it was still turning when the vessel came into contact with the reef. The massive rudder, however, broke clean away and is missing altogether. The absence of that rudder creates a great deal of space below the after-deck, which was occupied by some very large shoals of fish, who seem to have adopted this area as their new home.

From here, the only direction to take is up and, as we ascended, we caught a brief glimpse of a guitarfish. Then we were above the after-deck in 4-5m of water. All the usual fittings such as bollards, vents, railings – even a ladder – leading up out of the water, remain intact. Right in the middle, however, is a big deck-winch onto which are coiled large rope hawsers. It would seem that a ship of this size needed a little more than ordinary manpower when it came to berthing alongside.

Tucked away behind that winch is a large open deck hatch – about two metres square, which allows easy entrance for internal exploration. Down past the ladder, now redundant, we turned left, only to find a dark empty room with no exit. Retracing our steps, we then headed in the opposite direction. This revealed a series of rooms, all well lit by rows of brass portholes along the starboard bulkhead. With the sun shining directly onto that side of the ship, each porthole provided a sharp beam of light, like a row of large torches all flickering and pointing in the same direction.

We did not have time for a thorough examination of every room because we were quickly distracted from all else when we found a route through to the engine room. Here, we found evidence of damage. I am not expert on such matters and I can only surmise the damage was caused by the engines turning at full speed at the time of impact between

The *Million Hope* is only partially submerged and can be seen from several miles away.

the propeller and the reef. Nevertheless, the engines are all still here and require many hours of diving to thoroughly explore. Exit to the surface was well lit and easy to follow.

Back at the surface, I swapped cameras and headed back down to the ship in order to investigate her decks. It was a very interesting journey, but should only be undertaken when sea conditions are calm enough. Generally speaking, we began just in front of the bridge deck and main-tained an average depth of 5-8m as we inspected one feature after another. At the beginning, however, we did undertake a very thorough inspection of No. 5 Hold where we dropped down to the floor at 18m.

Each hold is wide open and cavernous, containing nothing more than one or two of the heavy metal hatch covers that once kept the cargo dry. It is fair to say, having seen one hold you've seen them all. The cranes, however, are especially fascinating. All four cranes were identical and each weighed several hundred tons. They comprise an upright crane with an enclosed cockpit and a heavy gantry – all fitted with wire hawsers. Although, we were visiting these in reverse order, they, like the ship's holds, are numbered from the bows. The gantry of No. 1 Crane has swung around and now faces aft. No. 2 Gantry is lowered and rests over the ship's port side – at the very end of which is a small colony of anthias. No. 3 is half-raised, facing starboard and, as already described, No. 4 has broken away and fallen to the seabed below where it rests against the ship's hull. Finally, we reached the foc'sle and whilst the approach was particularly interesting, the top of the foc'sle remains out of the water.

POSTSCRIPT – At over 16,000 grt, the *Million Hope* is one of the largest shipwrecks most scuba divers are ever likely to visit. Had she come to rest in 40m, she would undoubtedly have become one of the world's most outstanding dive sites. Having carefully inspected this wreck and considered her overall condition and attitude, I think the best is yet to come. She is a very big ship sitting upright with a significant list to port. Her entire starboard side is resting against a reef. Her decks are barely underwater and, above these are four massive cranes plus an equally massive bridge deck. Collectively, these structures weigh many hundreds of tons and are evenly spaced along the entire length of the ship. Below deck level there are tears right through the port side hull. I have come to the conclusion, therefore, there will come a time in the not-so-distant future when this vessel will fall over onto her port side and become completely enveloped by the sea. Should this happen – and sooner rather than later, the *Million Hope* will then provide a much better attraction for the visiting scuba diver.

The gantry from No. 2 Crane leans over the port side of the ship.
The very end of the crane is becoming colonised by reef fishes.

◆ Chapter III ◆

ZINGARA

(GPS: 28° 01·005N, 34° 29·600E)

THE SHIP – Built by VEB Schiffwerft in their Neptun yard at Rostock in the former East Germany, this general cargo vessel was launched as the *Kormoran* in 1963. In 1976 her name was changed to *Adamastos* and in 1980, another change of owners saw her renamed *Zingara*. A rather smart ship, her dimensions were 82.4m x 12.6m with a draught of 4.25m and a displacement of 1,582 grt. The *Zingara*'s hull was ice-strengthened and comprised two cargo holds in front of a bridge and engine room located at the stern. She was powered by a 6-cylinder diesel engine capable of producing 1,365 hp and a top speed of 12 knots. The *Zingara* was owned and operated by Montemare di Navigazione Spa and registered in Naples, at the time of her loss.

THE LOSS OF THE *ZINGARA* – The *Zingara* sailed from the Jordanian port of Aqaba on 21 August 1984 with a cargo of phosphate rock. The following day she ran aground on Laguna Reef, immediately north-east of Jackson Reef and was subsequently declared a constructive total loss.

`The *Zingara* as *Adamastos*. The new name had been painted over the original name of *Kormoran* on the ships' hull, but the original name was made of large raised steel letters and is still to be found on the wreck. (FotoFlite)

Two factors arising from the wrecking of this ship have given cause for considerable speculation. As already mentioned, ships are required to keep to the Right when passing through the Straits of Tiran. In this way, traffic leaving the Gulf of Aqaba and heading for the open Red Sea is required to take the Enterprise Passage to the west of those aforementioned four coral reefs which dominate the centre of the Straits. All charts and instructions to mariners clearly show these requirements. It was, therefore, somewhat strange to discover that the fully loaded Zingara - outbound from Aqaba, hit a reef on the eastern side of the Straits when her southerly course demanded a very different route altogether. Furthermore, this ship struck that shallow reef with such force and speed that her bottom was removed.

DIVING THE *ZINGARA* – Even with the name *Kormoran* permanently etched in large steel letters on her bows, the true identity of this ship remained a mystery for many years. One published report actually describes the *Kormoran* as a large bulk carrier and entirely separate from the *Zingara* which, the report describes, as being underneath the 16,000 tonne *Million Hope* on the other side of the Straits of Tiran – but that's a story for another day.

The way in which the *Zingara* was lost means that the wreck is very broken up. She is, however, one of those rare wreck sites where everything seems to be neatly laid out between bows and stern – as though deliberately arranged by some giant hand. Most interesting of all, every constituent part is still there. A small portion of the top of the stern breaks the surface and acts as an ideal marker for the start of each dive. In every direction the diver is treated to a magnificent underwater terrain of hard corals at their finest and many of these are now firmly attached to various wreck features. There are also some spectacular Napoleon Wrasse and we were treated to five incredible specimens plus a turtle on our very first dive.

The stern rests over on its starboard side at an angle of about 45 degrees. Railings and bollards still adorn the after-deck – below which the rudder and propeller are still in place, occupying a small hole about two metres or so deeper than the surrounding seabed. This relatively intact part of the wreck soon gives way to large sections of the ship no longer in their rightful place. Rounding the stern, we found the broken remains of the bridge deck and I was impressed by the sight of two very large brass portholes. It's always nice to dive any wreck which has not been looted.

Large steel plates lie across the seabed affording the best possible examination. A pair of deck winches lie upside down with hard coral having already become very firmly established. Over to the right, one of the

A closer view of the windlass found on the *Zingara*'s foc'sle.

The stern of the *Zingara* just touches the surface.

ship's two masts lie pointing away from what was once the starboard side, towards the open sea. Swimming gently on, we eventually found a very large section, upside down and raised above the seabed. This was part of the forward decks and is complete with handrails. This led immediately to the foc'sle. Altogether, this part creates a fascinating scene. It is almost as though the top of the ship had been removed from the hull and then laid perfectly on top of the reef – looking as though the rest of the ship was all still there. In short, the evidence on the seabed supports the fact that this vessel was driven on to the reef at full speed.

The two large windlasses, complete with anchor chains are all covered with varying degrees of hard coral growth. Over on the port side, sufficient of the bows below deck level exist to reveal most of the raised steel letters of the ship's original name. Although the letters A and N are either missing or obscured by coral, the word 'KORMOR' is easily found. Off to the starboard side, the forward mast lies across a gently sloping bed of coral. The bow and stern sections are undoubtedly the most photogenic aspects of the entire wreck which has a lot to offer the serious diver as a second or even third dive of the day following deeper dives elsewhere.

Portholes and other brass objects found all over the *Zingara* reveal a shipwreck which has never been looted.

POSTSCRIPT – The *Zingara* met her end in the most dangerous of circumstances. Either the Captain decided to save time and wrongly sought to use the eastern channel – against all oncoming traffic and was, therefore, piling on the speed in order to get through as quickly as possible, or he simply made a monumental error of navigation and thought he was elsewhere. The damage sustained to the *Zingara* stands as a lasting testament to the speed of that ship at the time of impact. That speed would undoubtedly have endangered the lives of all those on board and, for that reason, it is highly unlikely this was a deliberate act of wrecking. Whatever the truth, the *Zingara* remains where she fell and provides much for the diver to explore and enjoy.

· Chapter IV ·

THISTLEGORM

(GPS: 27° 48·849N, 33° 55·222E)

Of all the shipwrecks in the entire Red Sea, the *Thistlegorm* sits mast and funnel above all others. Such is the pulling power of this single shipwreck, she attracts more divers than any other underwater site anywhere in the world. In fact, the *Thistlegorm* has consistently remained the world's foremost diving attraction ever since she was re-discovered in the early 1990s.

THE SHIP – The *Thistlegorm* was a general cargo ship built by Joseph Thompson & Sons of Sunderland and launched in June 1940. She possessed five cargo holds; two fore, two aft and one (No. 3) below a central bridge deck. Above Nos 1, 2, 4 and 5 holds was a single Tween Deck. Her dimensions were 126.55m x 17.74m with a draught of 7.56m and a displacement of 4,898 grt. The *Thistlegorm* was powered by a 3-cylinder triple-expansion steam engine which generated a comfortable 365 hp and a top speed of 11 knots. She was one of a number of 'Thistle' ships owned and operated by the Albyn Line. With her construction being part-funded by the British government, however, she was destined for war duties from the moment she was launched.

The only known photograph of the *Thistlegorm* is of an imcomplete ship taken at her launching. This photograph is of one of her true sister ships, the Finnish vessel *Inkeri Nurminen*, which was built by J.L. Thompson in 1939 as the Argyll for the Sunderland Steamship Co. (World Ship Society)

Apart from the official photograph of her launching, there appears to be no pictures of the *Thistlegorm* from her days afloat. That said, it was Thompson & Sons who provided three prototype vessels which evolved into the famous Liberty ship – ships America built faster than U-Boats could sink them. No fewer than 2,710 Liberty ships were launched in a period of four years – one of which was built in a record four days. Many of these ships bear a striking resemblance to the *Thistlegorm*.

With a raised gun platform built over her stern, the *Thistlegorm* was immediately designated an armed freighter – although an overall shortage of weapons meant that only an old 4·7-inch gun and a heavy calibre machine gun, both of first world war vintage, were all that could be spared. Her maiden voyage was to the USA to collect steel rails and aircraft and her second voyage was to South America for grain. During this latter journey the captain decided on some mid-ocean gunnery practise.

The traversing mechanism of the 4·7-inch gun was badly worn and had been replaced with a manual mechanism which meant that one person had to push the barrel round by hand as it was being fired. The second round jammed in the breech. Such misfires are always dangerous, because an attempt to fire the round has been made and it can, therefore, now explode at any time. Consequently, a long rope was tied to the firing mechanism which led away to a shelter behind the aft mast house. The resultant flash engulfed the entire stern of the ship – with the projectile managing a whole fifty metres before dropping into the sea. With that, all gunnery practice ended.

The *Thistlegorm*'s third voyage was to the West Indies for a cargo of sugar and rum. This, however, culminated in a return to the Clyde where she was laid up for two months for repairs to her boilers before being assigned her final cargo.

THE LOSS OF THE *THISTLEGORM* – By May 1941, the Thistlegorm was in her home port of Glasgow being loaded with supplies essential for the British 8th Army and the relief of Tobruk. Described on the manifest as MT (Motor Transport), this broad description also included; Bren-carriers, BSA WD M20 motorcycles, generators, weapons, trailers, vehicle spares, aircraft parts (Blenheim bomber engine cowlings and tail-planes, Bristol Mercury engine cylinders and Westland Lysander wings), two RAF Pundit Ident Beacon trolleys, radios, land mines, shells, ammunition, rubber thigh-boots and I am indebted to Chris Frost - a diver from London, for identifying many of these items. To save cargo space, the motorcycles were placed onto the back of the trucks prior to loading. Two Stanier 8F 2-8-0 locomotives, two tenders and two water bowsers were also carried as deck cargo.

These locomotives were built by the North British Locomotive

Company of Glasgow and were standard War Department (WD) issue for the Royal Engineers. By the end of 1941, forty six of these locomotives had been shipped to Egypt, with only four being lost en route. Yet more were shipped out at later dates. In addition to Egypt, many of these engines went on to see service in Palestine, Iran and Iraq where they formed the bedrock for the fledgling state railways of those countries. Others were eventually sold to Italy and Turkey. In 1947, the War Department (now Ministry of Defence) sold thirty-nine surplus locomotives to London Midland Region – some of which survive to this day.

Because of her classification as an armed freighter, her Captain, William Ellis, had an additional team of nine Royal Navy personnel on board to man the guns. Thus it was that on 2 June 1941, Captain Ellis ordered the mooring lines slipped before easing his ship out of Glasgow, a port that neither the ship nor nine of those on board would ever see again. Sailing independently down the west coast of Britain, the *Thistlegorm* made good time to her secret rendezvous off the south coast of England. Here she joined a large convoy and, being armed, was assigned a prominent position towards the leading edge, by the Commodore. With Axis Forces occupying almost all of the northern Mediterranean coastline and Malta under constant siege, the safest route to Alexandria was via South Africa. This lengthy detour was uneventful. After refuelling in Cape Town, they were joined by HMS *Carlisle* – a light cruiser of 4,190 tons, before proceeding up the east coast of Africa and finally entering the Red Sea.

A Stanier 8F 2-8-0 locomotive similar to the two which were being carried as deck cargo on the *Thistlegorm*. Destined for military use in the Middle East, the locomotives on board the *Thistlegorm* were slightly modified by having 'cow catcher' life guards at the front of the engine. (Ian Morley)

The remains of one of the two Stanier 8F 2-8-0 Locomotives which were being carried as deck cargo on the *Thistlegorm*. This engine is found on the seabed off the port side of the wreck and, from this angle, looks deceptively intact. Note the 'cow catcher' life guards at the front of the engine.

An AEC Matador 4x4 Tractor Unit showing the standard bodywork for use when carrying equipment, munitions or personnel. (Imperial War Museum)

By the time they arrived at the entrance to the Gulf of Suez, it was the third week in September. The *Thistlegorm* was assigned immediately to Safe Anchorage F, to await further instructions. The master let out the starboard anchor and some 250 metres of chain, and allowed the gentle current to push the vessel back until he was satisfied all was well.

This was good holding ground and, at long last, the main engines were closed down. All they could do now was wait for clearance to proceed through the Suez Canal to Alexandria.

A BSA WD (War Department) M20 motorcycle. British industries produced 425,000 motor cycles for use by British and Allied troops during WW2. Of these, BSA produced 126,334 machines. (Henk Joore – BSA WD M20 Website)

An AEC Matador 4x4 Tractor Unit in the *Thistlegorm's* No. 2 Hold. Note also the aircraft engine cowling in the foreground.

These were difficult times. Getting through the canal was dependent on several factors: Enemy activity, especially air raids from German aircraft based in Crete; cargo priority, and how long other vessels had been waiting all had to be taken into consideration. At this time, however, two vessels had collided further up the Gulf and were virtually blocking the

Part of what is probably the world's largest collection of BSA WD M20 motorcycles. Souvenir-hunting divers have removed various items – a practise which now extends to collecting the spokes from the wheels...

canal's entrance. It was for this reason the *Thistlegorm* – with her much needed and valuable cargo, remained at anchor for a full two weeks. Up until now these safe anchorages, each with their own letter of the alphabet, were regarded as exactly that: Safe! There were no enemy ships or submarines and their aircraft rarely ventured this far south. This was all about to change. German Intelligence received information that a large troopship (possibly the *Queen Mary*) was due to travel through the Suez Canal with twelve hundred British troop reinforcements destined for North Africa.

Having mastered the relatively new skill of night flying, Heinkel He 111's from No. II/26 Kampfgeschwader (No. 2 Group, 26th Fighter Squadron), were alerted to the possible presence of a large vessel. Their task was to seek and destroy. At 22.50 hours on 5 October 1941, two twin-engine Heinkels crossed the north Egyptian coast heading south-east in search of this prize. Aided by a clear moonlit night they searched in vain for a big ship until fuel levels became critical. Then, just as they were on the point of returning home empty handed, one of the pilots spotted a ship at anchor. Turning away in order to put his aircraft in the best possible position for an attack, the pilot turned again as he continued to lose altitude. Coming in low over the sea and approaching the stern of the *Thistlegorm*, he released two bombs.

Both bombs penetrated No. 5 Hold – aft of the bridge, and detonated a great deal of ammunition. The resultant explosions sent the two loco-motives spiralling into the air as the ship was ripped open like a huge tin can. Even to this day, the rear decks from above No. 4 Hold are found peeled back towards the bridge, leaving many divers wondering what exactly they are looking at.

The vessel began to sink and the crew quickly abandoned ship. With hardly any time to launch the lifeboats, most of them leapt straight into the sea. One injured man however, was trapped on the blazing deck and desperately needed help. Crewman Angus McLeay wrapped some rags around his bare feet and ran across the hot steel plates and rescued him – an act for which the thirty-year-old from Stornoway was awarded the George Medal and Lloyd's War Medal for Bravery at Sea.

Caught unawares, the *Thistlegorm* had been given no time to defend herself and badly damaged, she quickly sank. The event was timed at 0130 hrs 6 October 1941. Captain Ellis and the other survivors were rescued by HMS *Carlisle* and taken to Port Tewfik (Suez), where he reported that four members of his crew of thirty-nine and five of the nine

Royal Navy ratings had lost their lives. Such was the part played by Captain Ellis in the evacuation of his ship and the saving of so many lives, he was subsequently awarded the OBE, for 'Services to the War Effort,' by King George VI. The spectacular loss of the *Thistlegorm*, however, had lit up the night sky, revealing more vessels at anchor to the retreating German aircraft. From that moment on, these hitherto safe anchorages would never be quite so safe again.

The heavy calibre machine gun found on the raised gun platform located immediately above the stern of the *Thistlegorm*.

(*Opposite*) At 01.30 hrs 6 October 1941, a German Heinkel He 111 aircraft from No. II/26 Kampfgeschwader attacked and sunk the *Thistlegorm*. The resultant explosion detonated some of the ammunition being carried as cargo in numbers 4 and 5 Holds. (Rico Oldfield)

The imposing bows of the *Thistlegorm*.

My diving partner swims towards the bows of the *Thistlegorm* along the starboard side of the wreck. To his left is one of the two Railway Tenders which were being carried as deck cargo and are located immediately in front of the bridge deck.

THE SHIP TODAY – For many years, British vessels passing the site where the *Thistlegorm* went down would dip their flags as a mark of respect to those who lost their lives. The ship itself, however, remained undisturbed until the early fifties when Jacques Cousteau explored her. He raised several items from the wreck – including one of the motorcycles, the captain's safe and the ship's bell. The February 1956 edition of *National Geographic* magazine clearly shows the ship's bell still in place and Cousteau's divers in the ship's lantern room – the contents of which were also still in place – but not, apparently, when the vessel was redis-covered by modern Scuba divers. Cousteau later published a book which did not reveal the exact position of the ship and once again, the *Thistlegorm* passed into obscurity. All that changed in the early nineties, when a group of divers happened upon her, by chance. In so doing, they had re-discovered one of the greatest shipwrecks of all time.

What makes this ship so extra-special is a combination of several fac-tors. To begin with, despite extensive damage aft of the bridge, for the main part, the ship is upright and on an even keel. Then, there is the story of her passing, with all the ingredients of war, heroism and tragedy – some-thing never re-created in a ship deliberately sunk for scuba diving. Then, prevailing conditions and accessibility all come into play and the Red Sea is hardly bleak and wind-swept. In other words, an acceptable climate and relatively warm waters, coupled with very good underwater visibility and a maximum depth of just 32m to the seabed all play their part.

And if anyone should enquire; 'What more could be asked of any ship-wreck?' the answer would be, 'its cargo!' In the case of the *Thistlegorm*, that cargo is a veritable underwater museum.

DIVING THE *THISTLEGORM* – I well remember my very first visit. My guide was called Ali Baba (yes – truly!) and was something of a celebri-ty. Deaf since birth, this man could lip-read in five languages and was an exceptionally fine diving guide/instructor with a great sense of humour. As our boat was being positioned above the *Thistlegorm*, Ali Baba was the first person into the water. He took a chain loop attached to a stout rope all the way down to the anchor chains at the bows while our skip-per kept way on the boat, to make his task easier. Captain Hassan is still widely regarded as the second-best captain in the entire Red Sea. Not that he minds, everyone acknowledges his father as the outstanding fig-ure in this regard as it was he who first located the *Thistlegorm* in 1963.

Boat secured, the engines were switched off and it was time for a most memorable encounter. We followed the rope halfway down before cross-ing to the bridge, just as soon as it came into view. From here we could see those WW2 vehicles on the starboard side of No. 2 Tweendecks – exactly as depicted in some of the many accounts I had studied. Below these was sufficient room to allow us to swim into the hold, over the tops of many more vehicles still parked as though, even now, they are waiting to be unloaded. Behind each cab, we found three motorcycles, stowed in this fashion purely for the sea passage. With the powerful lights from twin Ikelite strobes illuminating this incredible scene, it suddenly became all too obvious why so many downbeat articles have also been written about this outstanding shipwreck.

The motorcycles had been pushed over by divers searching for something to remove and keep. The badges, pedals, twist grips and tool kits were all gone. In some instances, they have also taken the spokes from the wheels. As for the lorries and trucks, there are only a few steering wheels left – but that was not all. In order to get at those steering wheels or, in some cases a souvenir from the engine, some divers had smashed their way in through the roof or bonnet, maximising the damage caused in search of their wretched trophy. So much for the cargo. The ship's brass fittings are also all long gone. Perhaps those writers who have had the temerity to publish photographs of these stolen goods have the answer… Strong words I know, but apart from breaking the laws of Egypt, this ship is also an unofficial war grave!

Over the years, however, even greater damage occurs each and every day – caused by the diving boats themselves. Anything up to twenty boats might be moored over the *Thistlegorm* at any one time. The first to arrive generally tie up to the shallower reaches of the wreck, such as the bridge. For the dive guide – who is the first into the water to secure the boat and then has to retrieve that mooring line at the end of the day's diving – the shallower the better. Then, when there is no more space, the boats tie up to each other. Some of the larger boats weigh several tons and it's easy to see how the combined force of such a small fleet – all pulling together as they take a single wave, is able to exert such pressures that no ship's superstructure was ever designed to withstand. In 1998, large sections of the *Thistlegorm*'s bridge were to be found on the seabed off the starboard side, with yet more, and even larger sections, hanging down and swaying precariously on the port side.

In 2000 I wrote: 'When I returned in 1999, the bridge section was even shorter and the large section that had been hanging down the side of the wreck was now residing on the seabed.' After yet another visit in early 2002, I discovered, to my horror, the roof of the bridge was no more. Incredible as it may sound, the roof of the bridge of the world's most outstanding shipwreck had been entirely ripped off during the preceding year. It remains the supreme irony that the world's foremost scuba diving attraction is literally being pulled apart by the very boats who are dependent on her for their livelihood.

Underneath the *Thistlegorm*'s foc'sle there are still new areas to explore.

This Bedford Truck from No. 1 Hold is one of many WW2 British military vehicles which are still found inside the *Thistlegorm*.

On the port side of No. 2 Hold are a small number of
RAF Pundit identification beacon trolleys.

Despite the manner of her sinking and the ongoing destruction, the
Thistlegorm is still in remarkable condition. The front section remains
largely intact and sits upright on a sandy seabed at a maximum depth of
32m. The starboard anchor is deployed, some railings are still in place

An RAF Pundit identification beacon trolley. From a small tower erected on
top of the main structure, a powerful light transmitted Morse-code signals
over great distances. By indentifying each unique signal, returning aircrew
were able to determine their precise location. (RAF Museum Cosford)

and all the winch houses, winches, blocks, windlasses and other paraphernalia are there to be investigated. From the bows, the diver drops
down from the foc'sle to the main deck and is immediately confronted by
two 4-wheeled railway water bowsers on either side of No. 1 Hold, with
the one on the port side resting precariously over the edge of the hold.
Either side of No. 2 Hold at deck level are the two railway tenders,
beside which are two torpedo-shaped Paravanes.

Each hold was built on two levels, with the upper level known as "tween
decks.' Throughout the ship, these decks provided additional cargo space
and several vehicles are still found here. Bedford trucks and a number of
motorcycles are found on the starboard side with RAF Pundit Beacon
Trolleys on the port side. Below this, is the main hold itself where much
of the cargo of parts and spares has come to look like an accumulation
of debris that serves to obscure much that might have been of interest –
including more vehicles, trapped beneath.

Dropping down into No. 2 Hold immediately in front of the bridge, and
heading over to the starboard side, there begins an incredible diving journey. Swimming gently above the vehicles, there is plenty of room to
explore and inspect the various lorries, trailers, motorcycles and other
items as you journey below and pass through No. 3 Hold deep inside the

The water carrier found on the foredeck on the port side of
No. 1 Hold, hangs precariously over that Hold. Note how this
bowser has been crushed by the pressure of water.

The *Thistlegorm* has become so popular with divers that several boats
are often moored directly onto the wreck itself.

ship. Here are the small arms – weapons of various calibre in packs of
ten, placed butt to muzzle with each pack now concreted together as a
single entity. Beyond this is the fuel store – virtually empty after such a
long journey. To one side, however, there is a large gap where the diver
is quite easily able to exit through the bulkhead which once formed the
outer wall of No. 4 Hold.

Emerging into the daylight, the diver is confronted by the devastation
that surrounded the sinking. Ammunition boxes form a large pile of fairly
uniform debris on top of which are some up-turned Bren carriers with
their characteristic tracks. Jutting out from the fore section is the broken drive shaft and some twenty metres further on is the remainder,
sticking out of what remains of the stern. Here is another Bren carrier
almost completely covered in debris and ammunition boxes. Nearby are a
number of very large shells, possibly fifteen inch and which were once
destined for a British Capital ship.

The stern itself is canted over at an angle of forty-five degrees and is
as interesting as any other part of the ship. Above the stern is the raised
gun platform with its two deck-mounted guns still in place. These are
best viewed from below where they make excellent silhouettes against the
distant surface. Below this platform, the vessel's rear accommodation
block is intact and rarely visited by divers.

Turning around and swimming above the wreck, the diver passes over
the most extensively damaged section once again before the forward section begins to take shape. Here is that upper deck which was peeled back
and now reaches almost to the bridge. The evenly-spaced steel girders
which once supported the deck are now on top, and who knows what lies
trapped below? Off the port side, one can also see the remains of one of
the two railway engines, sitting upright on the seabed. The other is also
sitting upright and is found off the starboard quarter. A gentle current
generally prevails from bow to stern. Large grouper, blacktip sharks,
jacks and tuna are amongst the largest fish to be encountered, with the
latter two species providing an early morning display of speed and agility
as they attack shoals of smaller fish at breakfast time. Most, if not all, of
the common reef fishes are also in evidence.

POSTSCRIPT – From a diver's viewpoint, what makes a good shipwreck
is largely dependent on the individual. Few, however, would disagree that
the *Thistlegorm* is amongst the very best and, as I have said, stands mast
and funnel above all others. After carefully considering both the state of
the ship (at least, as it was) and the cargo she still carries, it is easy to
see why this particular vessel was catapulted from obscurity to become
the world's foremost diving attraction, virtually overnight. The mighty
Thistlegorm is a legend amongst divers and her place will be enshrined
forever in diving's own Hall of Fame. In the meantime, however, she has
become a victim of her very own status and remains in serious decline.
Sadly, none of us shall ever see this shipwreck as good as she was on the
day she was re-discovered – only a few short years ago. How long she can
now last as a leading diving attraction, is anybody's guess. I do believe
that without this wreck, diving tourism in Egypt would enter into serious
decline.

• Chapter V •

KINGSTON

(GPS: 27° 46·686N, 33° 52·551E)

THE SHIP – Built in Sunderland by the Oswald Shipbuilding Company, the *Kingston* was launched on 16 February 1871. Technically, described as an 'iron screw brigantine', this general cargo vessel possessed 2 cargo holds – one fore and one aft. This was a relatively new breed of ship which was still distrusted by many of the sea-hardened master mariners of the day because she had a funnel in addition to more conventional sail. Powered by a single, coal-fired 2-cylinder compound steam-engine which produced a very creditable 130 hp, the *Kingston* was capable of a top speed of 11 knots. Her dimensions were 78m x 10m with a draught of 6m and a displacement of 1,449 grt. The ship was owned and operated by the Commercial Steamship Company at the time of her loss.

HISTORICAL CONTEXT – It was during the 1840s that the first screw propellers were perfected and, whilst sail would still remain a feature for many years to come, the coal-fired steam engine had arrived. Being at the head of a huge empire, Britain soon became heavily committed to a programme of building steam-powered commercial and battle fleets in

An artist's impression of the *Kingston*. Almost the entire history of the Oswald Shipbuilding Company of Sunderland, England was lost during WW2. There are no known photographs of the *Kingston*. This picture was compiled after extensive research by both the author and artist. (Rico Oldfield)

order to serve and protect her many outposts. Whilst there were always those who criticised this new means of propulsion, this was a time of revolution in both ship design and building techniques. By December 1869, a whole new class of ironclad – in the form of HMS *Warrior*, was launched on the Thames. The pace of change however was to continue, as each new class of warship was all too quickly outpaced and outgunned by newer, bigger and faster vessels. This naval arms race of the new industrial age would eventually climax in the era of the Dreadnought battleship itself.

This background is relevant for two reasons. Firstly, individual improvements being made to marine engines were being published almost daily and quite naturally, picked up and adopted or adapted by the shipbuilding industry. Secondly, the one commodity needed by all steamships, with their fancy 'SS' prefix, was coal and delivering that commodity would eventually become the destiny of the *Kingston* and many ships like her.

Naturally, there were also those who readily embraced the new technology, but whatever the individual preference, even the staunchest enemies of change could not help but admire the *Kingston*'s fine lines. When sailing before the wind, this schooner-rigged steamship cut a dashing figure with her fore-mast displaying fore-sail, fore-gaff topsail, jib, flying jib and fore-stay sail and her main-mast sporting main-sail and main gaff topsail. As with all these new steamships, however, a combination of using power and sail often led to an unkempt appearance with soot staining all sails aft of the funnel – and occasionally even setting them alight.

By early 1881, the *Kingston* was approaching her tenth birthday and had been employed on collier duties for the previous two years. She undertook regular runs to the Mediterranean, the Middle East and beyond. Her task being to fill the coal storage bunkers of the many ports she visited so that other visiting steamships were able to refuel there.

THE LOSS OF THE *KINGSTON* – On the morning of 28 January 1881, Captain Thomas Cousins paced the decks continually studying his pocket watch. He was familiar with the port of Cardiff and wanted to make the best possible use of the tide. Once again he checked his watch and, just as soon as his vessel lifted from the seabed, they would depart. Suddenly the boat moved and all hands went into action. Cousins barked a succession of orders and, as the mooring lines were slipped, he duly pulled away from the wharf – destination Aden.

Cousins was a man of considerable experience of the sea. At the age of eighteen he had rounded the Cape in a Force 12 gale. He had repeated the experience on more than one occasion and gone aloft to furl the sails with frozen hands while he was about it. Despite all his experience, however, Cousins was a man who was prone to making the occasional mistake.

Viewed from off the starboard side, the stern of the
Kingston dwarfs my fellow scuba divers.

Looking down onto the after-deck of the *Kingston* immediately above the stern.

He was very lucky to get away with having caused a collision whilst in charge of his first command (the *Harrington)* and had grounded the *Kingston,* although it was successfully refloated two days later. These errors had not gone unnoticed. His one redeeming feature, however, was that he was a very hard man and an imposing figure of over six feet (1.8m) tall, against whom few would dare argue.

It was a fine, fresh spring morning as they motored gently out in to the mouth of the Severn against the incoming tide, at less than 5 knots. Once into the Bristol Channel, the captain recognised a favourable wind and duly ordered all sails set as they headed south for the Bay of Biscay. The weather was good and the wind was kind and it was not long before they reached warmer climes – something that always made sailing before a good breeze a great joy. The use of sail saved the owners a great deal of money in fuel and most masters did their best in this respect. Being under constant sail, all day and night, however, was very tiring for the crew.

Spring was always regarded as the best time to sail through the Mediterranean and, as the days passed, they continued to average a steady 6-7 knots. Eventually Port Said came within sight and the engines roared into life as the sails were furled and the pilot cutter came alongside. The first mate also held a master's ticket but had yet to secure a command. The owners had told him that a spell under Cousins would teach him much about being at sea – though the lessons that fate had in store would be very different from those that were intended.

The *Kingston* finally cleared Suez on 20 February 1881 and the sails remained furled as Cousins began to negotiate the narrow waters of the upper reaches of the Straits of Suez. These were dangerous and if he had trusted his first mate a little more things might have turned out differently. As the hours passed, Cousins had little or no rest as he continued to navigate by himself. Not once did he ask any of his officers to check his calculations or bearings. So many hours of relentless concentration demanded the highest levels of physical strength and endurance. Then he made a mistake. He failed to ascertain the ship's correct position in relation to the Ghârib and Ashrafi lighthouses. Eventually the *Kingston* came to be much further to the east than he realised. Finally, it seemed to Cousins that the Gulf of Suez was about to widen as they approached the open Red Sea and, thinking the dangerous waters were almost passed, he relaxed. It was now dark and he gave instructions to his first mate, before retiring to his cabin.

A short time later, in the early hours of 22 February – almost exactly ten years to the day after the *Kingston* was launched, the ship ran aground on Shag Rock. Within moments, Cousins was back on the bridge and had taken charge. His first duty was to conduct all the usual internal and external checks of the hull and assess the overall condition of his ship. Early indications were that the *Kingston* had sustained little damage and that little or no water was being taken on. Regarding the incident as nothing more than another unfortunate grounding, Cousins posted various lookouts and watches before waiting to seek help from any passing ship.

It was not quite daybreak when the lights of a British steamship came into view and quickly responded to the rocket fired to attract her attention. Unable to render assistance himself, however, the master agreed to make all haste for Suez and send assistance. That ship then promptly departed just as quickly as he had arrived.

The Times dated 25 January 1881, carried the following item:

'WRECKS AND CASUALTIES

Lloyd's agent at Suez telegraphs that the *Kingston*, British steamer, is ashore at Suez and is leaking a little. Assistance has been sent.'

This was hardly a cause for concern for anyone with an interest in either the ship, her cargo or her crew but, by the time it was published, 'leaking a little' was already much worse. Throughout the 23rd, Cousins continued to assess the state of his ship and it soon became quite clear she was 'down by the stern'. By the afternoon of the second day, Cousins had the ship's boats made ready and launched, ordering they remain alongside and ready until the last possible moment. Eventually all power and

Situated on one of the finest hard-coral reefs I have ever seen, the fish life on the wreck of the *Kingston* is quite outstanding.

The *Kingston*'s port quarter showing the stern bollards.

light was lost as the water reached the engine room. Cousins ordered every man into the boats and to stand off a short distance from the ship. Knowing that help would not be long in arriving, Cousins remained on the *Kingston* until the last possible moment before leaping into one of the boats just as his ship suddenly settled by the stern. He could only turn and watch as the *Kingston* slipped gracefully back from the reef which had proved her undoing until only the masts were visible above the surface. The lifeboats then tied up to those masts and it was here that captain and crew were found, less than two hours later. No injuries were sustained.

An Egyptian salvage tug and two lighters had been dispatched to the site to salvage the cargo. On discovering the vessel to be sunk, however, there was nothing to be done and no salvage was ever made. The master of the salvage ship reported his findings to the ship's owners and the *Kingston* was duly abandoned as a constructive total loss on 28 February 1881.

THE LEGEND OF *SARAH H* – On first being discovered, the *Kingston* became known as the *Sara H*, even though there has never been a shipwreck of that name. Many years ago, underwater photographer and author Shlomo Cohen, spent several weeks working in and around the Sinai Peninsula writing his excellent *Red Sea Diver's Guide*. Towards the end of this endeavour, he came across a shipwreck on Shag Rock which

was hitherto unknown. That wreck was the *Kingston*. One version of events is that nobody on board his boat had any idea of the ship's name, history or even nationality. As the wreck had been underwater for so long, there was no chance of anyone having any knowledge of her loss. Cohen needed to give the vessel a working name; not uncommon by any means. He was working from the *Mv Sea Surveyor* – a dive boat owned and operated by David Hillel, whose charming wife, Sarah, was the resident dive-master. Consequently, it was suggested that the unknown wreck be named in honour of her and more credibility was added by including the H from her surname. Another version was that the ship's true name was already well-known to those on board, except Shlomo Cohen, and the crew played a joke by informing him the vessel was called the *Sarah H*. Either way, such was the credibility of this name – especially that post-nominal 'H', that even today there are those who still insist on calling the *Kingston* by a name that never was.

DIVING THE *KINGSTON* – The *Kingston* sits upright on an even keel with her bows smashed into the reef. From time to time, when strong currents are present, it is generally better to start with an inspection of the propeller and rudder at 17m on the seabed. After this, the diver needs to swim upwards and into the remains of the wreck itself. After more than one hundred and twenty years underwater, the *Kingston* is in remarkable condition. Just less than half of the hull from amidships to

The Crow's Nest on the *Kingston*'s mainmast which lies
on the seabed off the starboard side of the wreck.

Below the ship's steel framework and accumulated debris,
the diver will find the *Kingston*'s cargo of coal is still intact.

POSTSCRIPT – Thomas Richards Cousins was born in Portsmouth in 1836 and gained his Master's Certificate in Dundee in 1876. After previous spells as first mate on the *Harrington* and the *Tynemouth Castle*, the *Harrington* became his first command before he was appointed to the *Kingston* in April 1880. His record of service shows the *Harrington* to have been in collision with another vessel in April 1878 and the *Kingston* to have previously run aground at Bolderaa in September 1880. After the loss of the *Kingston*, Cousins was adjudged to have been negligent and his Master's Certificate was suspended for six months from 13 April 1881. He was then given command of the *Harvest* in October 1881, and promptly ran her aground the following month. This happened again one month later and yet again in December 1882. After then receiving a very stern warning from the ship's owners, he promptly settled down to complete a full and fruitful career at sea without further mishap.

the stern is still fairly intact. The weight of the cargo keeps everything in place and has prevented the vessel from being pushed over by currents.

Immediately above the stern are the remnants of a tiller, below which the rudder post disappears through the decks. Nearby is evidence of a number of very small portholes having been removed. The wooden decks have rotted away, leaving a series of steel spars and beams, on top of which sits the ship's spare propeller. The wreck is wide open allowing the diver to descend to two levels beneath the beams – although there are no enclosed spaces. The cargo of coal is intact, but with coral growth over the surface it is not immediately obvious as such. Amidships was where the engine room was located and proved to be the weakest part of the ship when under stress. This is well broken-up although various fittings and a large boiler are still available for inspection. The front half of the ship is nothing more than a collection of large pieces of debris scattered across a coral slope. The ship's masts are found on the seabed off the starboard side.

This corner of Shag Rock is home to one of the most incredible stretches of hard-coral coastlines I have ever seen. That same coral has also colonised the wreck. All the local reef fishes are present and combine to make this a fabulous wreck – a splendid second, or even third, dive after a much deeper visit to the *Thistlegorm* earlier in the day. The wreck is, altogether, quite excellent.

Chapter VI

DUNRAVEN

(GPS: 27° 42·190N, 34° 07·355E)

THE SHIP – Built by Mitchell & Company of Newcastle-upon-Tyne and launched in December 1873, the *Dunraven* was officially described as an 'iron screw steamer, planked' and possessed 2 cargo holds – one fore and one aft. This was another of that relatively new breed of ship which could choose either sail or steam. In this case she was Topsail-Schooner rigged and could sport 2 square-rigged topsails, 2 staysails and a foresail from the fore-mast in addition to mainsail, main staysail and gaff topsail from the mainmast at the rear. Below decks she was fitted with a coal-fired 2-cylinder compound inverted steam engine capable of producing 140 hp and a top speed of 8 knots (unladen). This was made by Messrs Humphrys and Tennant also of Newcastle. Her dimensions were 79.6m x 9.8m with a draught of 7.3m and a displacement of 1,613 grt. She was owned and operated by W. Milburn of London and, after completion of successful sea trials, was immediately employed on the Bombay run.

WHO WAS FIRST? – Curiously, the *Dunraven* is not marked on any Admiralty chart. One published account of the discovery of this wreck states that in 1977, a German geologist came across the wreck whilst undertaking survey work for an oil company. Although he passed on what

The original builder's plan of the *Dunraven*. There are no known photographs of the ship. (Tyne and Wear Archives)

little information he had collected to the owner of a local diving facility, his co-ordinates were, apparently, so vague, the vessel was not found again for more than another two years. Another account dismisses the 'geologist' story as being deliberately created to lessen the achievement of those who did discover the wreck.

What is fact, is that in the early 1970s, Howard Rosenstein formed Red Sea Divers and chose Na'ama Bay on the Sinai Peninsula for his base. In 1977 he decided on a course of action that would attract visitors away from more popular destinations, towards his corner of the Red Sea. His plan was to embellish history by inventing fictional connections with Lawrence of Arabia and his fabled treasure ships. Howard had been influenced by a newly released movie called *The Deep*, in which the wreck of the *Rhône* in the British Virgin Islands was featured. Having started on this course of action, all he needed was a suitable shipwreck.

Later that same year, he began to investigate information given to him by local Bedouin fishermen. Their directions were very easy to follow: 'There is a place out in the Gulf in the direction of the setting sun, far from land and at least three cigarettes from Râs Mohammed. Here there is a reef which comes out from the sea to break the surface at low tide. Go the end of this reef coming from the south east.' In Howard's own words: 'We broke out the charts and tried to sort this out – and from the various hints and markings, we just guessed at the final spot. Jumping into the water right on top of it [the wreck] was just a matter of luck. I had a group of American divers led by Carl Roessler of Sea and Sea fame as witnesses. I took a risk and it paid off.'

The shipwreck they had discovered was the *Dunraven* and whilst two more years would pass before she was correctly identified, she was of a type of ship that entirely suited Howard's purposes, and allowed him to elaborate on that Lawrence of Arabia connection. The next development came from the BBC who wanted to make a programme about the wreck. Naturally, whilst working on various theories about the ship's identity, Howard deliberately stepped up his campaign about the connection with the legendary Lawrence, who had used a number of different vessels to move valuable treasure from Suez to Aqaba, in order to finance the Arab revolt against the Turks. These ships were, apparently, the *Dufferin*, *Harding*, *M-31* and *Suva* – some of which were very similar in design to the *Dunraven*. It was not long before rumours began to circulate about the possibility of divers having found one of Lawrence's lost treasure ships. Now, over 25 years later, Howard Rosenstein is happy to admit that he deliberately planted this notion of a connection with history. That inventiveness, however, was a vital tool in getting the required recognition for his corner of the Red Sea and, not only did it work, but the rest, as they say, is history. Just visit Na'ama Bay and you will see what I mean.

A view of the stern of the *Dunraven*.

Eventually, of course, everyone became aware of the ruse and any connection with Lawrence came to an end. Even so, one fanciful rumour was then quickly replaced by another when it was suggested that the vessel might be a mysterious Q ship that had been sent to the Middle East during World War 1 on a secret mission, and during which the vessel was alleged to have disappeared. It was all more great fiction and doubtless enjoyed as stories continued to circulate.

Finally, in November 1979, the name *Dunraven* was found engraved on some fine porcelain and whilst this initially led researchers in several different directions as they tried to determine precisely which *Dunraven* it was, the ship was soon correctly identified. Further confirmation was also obtained when Howard and his divers cleaned the lettering on the stern of the vessel using a pneumatic wire brush. This operation can be seen in the resultant BBC film, *The Mystery of the Red Sea Wreck*, screened in late 1979 as part of the 'The World About Us' series. The BBC's own research also confirmed the name.

And, as if this discovery was not enough, all this was going on at the same time as the Camp David Peace Process. Having, therefore, invented a false but nevertheless intriguing connection with one era of Arabian history, suddenly the shipwreck became a small part of the region's modern history. The US ambassador to Israel, Samuel Lewis, returned from the Camp David talks and decided to participate in the BBC film and this

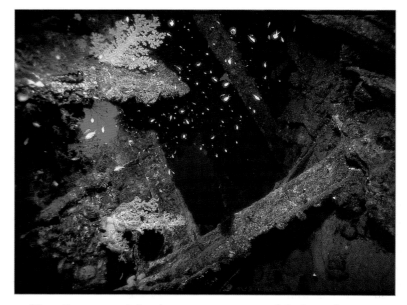

The collapsing – and thus dangerous – structures of the forward section.

resulted in Howard Rosenstein being told – on film, of the decision to return the Sinai Peninsular to Egypt. So, just as Howard was to achieve the ultimate success and international media coverage for his great discovery, being an Israeli, he was also being told he was about to lose his life's dreams and achievements.

THE LOSS OF THE *DUNRAVEN* – In January 1876, twenty-seven-year-old Captain Edward Richards Care supervised the loading of his ship in Liverpool. It was general cargo, which included timber and steel for India's fledgling industrial ambitions. The trip out to Bombay was without incident and by the end of March they were loading the *Dunraven* for the return leg. Eventually, the ship left Bombay on 6 April 1876 loaded with what was later described as a 'valuable general cargo bound for Liverpool.' The ship had a complement of twenty five.

They made good time across the Indian Ocean and, after a brief stop at Aden for coal, continued on and up through the Red Sea. On 24 April, the ship's log recorded 'weather fine and clear, wind light, water smooth, no sail set, vessel proceeding at full speed of six knots.' At 01.00 hrs the next morning the second mate saw high land right ahead and took this to be Shadwan Island. Fifty minutes later he saw a light which he took to be Ashrafi Light – way up in the Straits of Gobal. The master was on the Bridge throughout this time and never questioned either the sightings or their identification. The second mate described the light as a 'bright fixed light,' although he did later change his mind.

At 02.15 hrs, the master went below leaving orders to be called in one hour. Then, at 02.40 hrs, the light was lost to view – as though it had simply gone out. Once again, the later testimony of the second mate became confusing as he gave his evidence to the Enquiry. Firstly, he stated he called the master as soon as he lost sight of the light but later changed this to having called the master sometime between 03.30 and 03.40 hrs, thus admitting he had failed to follow orders. When Captain Care did arrive on deck, however, land was plain to see some seven miles off the starboard side to the north. It was now 03.40 hrs and immediately Care altered course two points to starboard. Curiously, this was closer to that land. Ten minutes later the look-out saw a large dark object in the water which he thought to be a buoy and called this out to the Bridge but got no reply. At the same instant, however, the second mate also saw the object but, thinking it was a boat, only casually reported it to the master. Care immediately ordered the engines stopped but before this could happen the *Dunraven* struck hard and the rocks immediately penetrated the forward hold.

Steam pumps were set to work and a fruitless attempt was made to heave her off by means of a kedge anchor. By 07.00 hrs, however, the water had reached the engine room and put out the fires. By midday the starboard side upper deck was under water and the master and crew took to the lifeboats. They remained with their doomed vessel until 16.00 hrs when a dhow came alongside and took the shipwrecked mariners on board. It was only now that the master of the *Dunraven* was made aware if his actual position – off the southern tip of the Sinai Peninsula.

The master later recorded that, at 5pm the *Dunraven* slipped off the reef and sank in 15 fathoms (27m). For three days the dhow remained at anchor over the *Dunraven* until Captain Care and his crew were transferred to the passing Italian steamer, *Arabia*, which conveyed them to Suez. The Peninsular and Oriental Steam Navigation Company's *Malwa* later transported the crew safely back to England.

Many divers enjoy swimming through the wreck of the *Dunraven* by entering at the stern and leaving the wreck after passing the engine room.

The resultant Board of Trade Enquiry heard conflicting evidence from both Captain Care and the second mate, with the master attributing the loss of his vessel to a combination of the Ashrafi Light going out and a stronger current than normal setting his vessel towards the reef. Nevertheless, the ship's log – always taken as an accurate record of

One of the many features found inside the engine room of the *Dunraven*.

events and in which all seemingly minor occurrences (bearings, sightings etc.) are always recorded as a matter of routine, made no mention of these concerns. This, in spite of the fact it had been written up some fourteen days after the sinking, when considerable thought would have been given to what was to be included.

In giving his judgement, Stipendiary Magistrate J. A. Yorke stated that 'the facts proved that the master had made no real efforts to ascertain by observation or otherwise the real position of the *Dunraven* after midday on 24 April and before striking at 03.50 on the 25th. The neglect of this most necessary precaution seems to have mainly caused the loss in question. Furthermore, it seems plain from careful examination of the chart produced that the land seen by the second mate could not have been Shadwan Island nor could the light have been from Ashrafi as asserted. In all probability it was merely the light of a passing vessel.'

Consequently, the Court found the loss of the *Dunraven* was caused by the default and negligence of the Captain and subsequently revoked his Master's Certificate for a period of twelve months with immediate effect, though allowing him a first mate's ticket during the time of suspension.

DIVING THE *DUNRAVEN* – The *Dunraven* is completely upside down and is found with her port side running parallel to an adjacent reef. At a depth of 17m, the top of the upturned bows are the shallowest part of the wreck with the stern resting on the seabed at 30m. The leading edge of the bows are broken and slightly separated, with the whole of the forepart structure leaning backwards and resting against the reef. From the port hawse pipe – almost completely hidden between ship and reef, the anchor chain runs down to the seabed and disappears under the ship. From the starboard hawse pipe is a short piece of anchor chain on which there is considerable coral growth. There is sufficient damage to the hull to allow the diver to enter the foc'sle – but only just. From the bows, it is a long swim above the upturned keel to a point approximately amidships where the hull is broken and the remains of the funnel lie on the seabed nearby. Here are often found a pair of large red scorpionfish.

At the break in the hull, it is tempting to try and enter the front section of the wreck – although this is not recommended. Here the keel is also broken and this has allowed the front half of the hull to collapse. With the break being immediately in front of the Engine Room, the ship's two huge boilers support the remainder of the hull and keel allowing it to retain its original shape. This is where the best part of the overall dive begins.

Surrounding the boilers are thousands of glassfish (Vanikoro sweepers) – a species which always prefer the shade and, on entering the hull, they move lazily aside to allow the diver safe passage. The boilers are side by

There is a large break in the hull of the *Dunraven* approximately amidships and this is where a pair of very large Red Scorpionfish are frequently found.

peared altogether, leaving little more than a metre of mast pointing to the cross-trees some distance away on the seabed.

Overall, the *Dunraven* provides the diver with a thoroughly enjoyable series of dives on one of Egypt's most famous shipwrecks. That said, as I have mentioned before, ships were never built to withstand the pressures exerted by the weight of their own structure except when found perfectly upright. Being upside down, the *Dunraven* is deteriorating faster than if she had been sitting upright on the seabed. That upside down structure cannot, therefore, be regarded as safe – and even if she is safe today, tomorrow might easily be very different. Please be warned.

POSTSCRIPT – Edward Richards Care (the second Christian name is not mis-spelled and it is simple coincidence that both Captain Cousins and Captain Care had this same middle name) was born in St. Ives in 1849 and gained his Master's Certificate (No. 88154) in London in 1872 at the very early age of twenty-three years. He was immediately assigned command of the *Etna* and later the *Alveaga* before taking over the *Dunraven* in August 1874. After its loss, however, it was not until 1877 that he returned to sea as a Captain – once again in command of the *Etna*. He then went on to complete a full career as a master mariner without further mishap.

side and although they occupy a large amount of space, there is plenty of room for single-file swimming between boiler and starboard side, right through to the stern. On the other side of the boilers are all the pipes, taps, valves and, of course, the engine itself, with large connecting rods and pistons all still in place. Above is a large gear wheel and even more valves. From this point, the view towards the stern can be quite breath-taking. This is a large, empty space with plenty of natural light provided by rows of portholes illuminating what was the starboard quarter. Altogether, this space allows considerable scope for photography.

With the deck having become the ceiling, the propeller shaft runs along it. Incredibly, after so long underwater, wooden panels still line this part of the steel hull. Sadly, however, all the ship's brass fittings, including the many portholes that once lined both sides of the ship at this point, were removed long ago. Such greed does, of course, lessen the overall effect for those of us who can only follow those who helped themselves and thought only of their own wretched trophy hunting!

Exit from the stern is well lit. This is at 30m and the deepest part of the dive. Once outside, on top of the hull, the rudder and propeller are still in place, although one of the four blades is missing. There is plenty of coral growth on the upturned hull, though not as prolific as one might expect on a vessel that has been underwater for such a length of time. Swimming back along the starboard side, the diver will find some remains of the aft mast. Most of the structure has, however, now disap-

Chapter VII

ULYSSES

(GPS: 27° 41·202N, 33° 48·128E)

THE SHIP – Yet another ship from Newcastle-upon-Tyne, the *Ulysses* was built by A. Leslie *&* Co. and launched in 1871. Officially described as an 'iron screw cargo steamer, planked,' she possessed 3 cargo holds – two fore and one aft. A fairly large boat for her day, her dimensions were 95.1m x 10.2m with a draught of 7.7m and a displacement of 1,992 grt. Like the *Dunraven*, she was Topsail-Schooner rigged and was, therefore, able to display the same configuration of sails. Below her centrally placed funnel was a 2-stroke, 2-cylinder coal-fired steam engine, also made in Newcastle by P. Stephenson *&* Co. This provided the ship with 225 hp and a top speed of 8 knots. The ship was owned and operated by the Ocean Steamship Company at the time of her loss.

To some, these relatively new 'steam and sail' vessels were nothing more than hybrids because they were neither one type of ship nor the other, and it is true that many possessed the worst possible sea-keeping qualities. The *Ulysses*, however, was a well made vessel, though perhaps a little unlucky.

THE LOSS OF THE *ULYSSES* – The island of Gobal Seghir (little Gobal) lies almost at the very end of the busy shipping lane which takes its name

The *Nestor*, one of seven sister ships built for the Anchor Line along with the *Diomed, Hector, Menelaus, Priam, Sarpedon* and *Ulysses*. (National Maritime Museum)

from the island's big brother. The Straits of Gobal are found at that point where the north-west Red Sea begins to narrow until it becomes the Gulf of Suez. Approaching from the other direction, the Straits come at a time when many ships' masters just out of Suez, have relaxed, thinking the more hazardous stretches of water are now behind them. But, they are not – as many have discovered to their cost. Today there are radar reflectors and solar-powered lights, but over one hundred years ago, things were very different indeed. In 1869 the Suez Canal was opened and immediately the Red Sea presented new experiences and very new lessons for many a seasoned ship's master. Many of these had never encountered coral reefs, which now lurked menacingly below the surface. Even today, these are hazardous waters. Imagine how treacherous they must have been then!

It was a beautiful morning in early August 1887 as Captain Arthur Bremner paced the decks of his beloved *Ulysses*, repeatedly pausing to study his pocket watch. Above him, the tall building proclaimed EAST INDIA TRADING COMPANY and, although that company had long ceased to exist, Bremner often found himself loading at their old warehouses right in the heart of London. As he checked his watch again, he studied the Thames. He wanted to make the best possible use of the ebb tide and at long last, it was time to depart. Suddenly, he barked a succession of orders and, as the mooring lines were slipped, he duly set sail. Destination Penang.

The *Ulysses* was a sturdy vessel with proud lines and unlike many 'steam and sail' ships of the period, responded well to either form of power. With a following wind to see them safely down the Thames, none would have guessed that this would prove to be the last voyage for this brave yet ill-fated little ship which, in the sixteen years since her launch, had enjoyed something of a chequered career. Bremner was a big man. Hardened by many years at sea, he was not a man to be challenged. Unfortunately, he was not exactly the ablest of ships' captains and was prone to making mistakes. Nevertheless, he did not lack courage and in 1884, whilst master of the *Nevada*, was awarded the Lloyd's Medal for saving life at sea. Bremner was also a stubborn man, always determined to prove himself.

Since 1880, he had commanded a succession of vessels but this would be his first visit to the Red Sea. Consequently, he spent much of his time checking every single aspect of his ship. Only when they were within the wide open stretches of the Atlantic and later, the Mediterranean, did he allow the first mate to exercise any control. It was a long and uneventful journey to Port Said where, all of a sudden, Bremner was very much in demand as he attended to customs officials, port authorities and pilots – dealing with all the rules, regulations and paperwork that went with the

After more than 120 years underwater, the *Ulysses'* wooden decking
has rotted away revealing a framework of steel girders.

job. From Port Said, however, he could relax a little as he allowed the
pilot to negotiate the two-hundred mile journey to Suez. Having cleared
that port, the pilot was dropped and Bremner checked their position. He
then plotted his course carefully before issuing some very definite and
very clear instructions. Had he been more approachable, things might
have turned out differently, but as the many hours passed, this ship's master simply wanted nothing more than to see his instructions closely followed.

By the evening of 15 August 1887, the *Ulysses* had almost completed
the entire length of the Gulf of Suez and was approaching the wider, and
much easier to navigate, open Red Sea. Feeling somewhat relieved the
dangerous waters were now behind him, a very tired Captain Bremner
checked his charts one last time before retiring to his cabin. In the early
hours of the 16th, however, the *Ulysses* struck Gobal Seghir. Bremner's
first duty was to conduct a thorough check, both internal and external,
of every single aspect of his ship's condition. At first it seemed the damage was slight and the pumps could easily handle the small amount of
water being taken on. Regarding the incident as nothing more than an
unfortunate grounding, Bremner decided to wait and seek help from the
first passing ship. Just before daybreak the lights of the British *Kerbela*
were sighted and she quickly responded to the rocket fired to attract her
attention. Unable to render assistance himself, the master of the *Kerbela*
agreed to make all haste for Suez and send immediate help.

The Times dated 18 August 1887, carried the following item:

'WRECKS AND CASUALTIES:
Lloyd's agent at Suez telegraphs that the *Kerbela*, British steamer,
reports that the *Ulysses*, British steamer, is ashore at Jubal (sic) Island,
and is leaking a little. Assistance has been sent.'

This was hardly a cause for concern to anyone reading the item but, on
board the ship, that 'leaking a little' had already become much worse.
Bremner had continually assessed the situation throughout that first day.
The *Ulysses* was stuck fast on a coral reef just north of Bluff Point.
Everything indicated minor leaking coupled with a slight worsening in
weather conditions and an equally slight increase in the sea state.
Bremner, however, was convinced his ship was not lost and decided
against dumping any cargo overboard in the belief his vessel would eventually be pulled free.

It was not until the 18th, however, that the owner's agents were able
to despatch that much needed assistance. In the meantime, Bremner continued to completely underestimate the power of a coral reef to inflict
damage on a steel-hulled vessel. Having already refused to jettison any

cargo, the fully laden *Ulysses* gently pivoted on a coral head and slowly 'worked the reef'. Consequently, the leaks increased until there was no option but to take appropriate action.

Finally, the crew began by dumping part of the cargo in shallow water from where it could be recovered once assistance arrived. No sooner was this done, however, than separate parties of armed Arabs and Maltese raiders landed on the otherwise deserted island and began plundering the jettisoned cargo. Bremner then decided no more cargo would be removed from the ship for the time being and that water levels would be continually monitored. Throughout all this time, the ship continued to steadily rock to and fro on a coral head in that increased sea state. This unrelenting process was weakening the hull of the ship and, without considerably lightening the load on that hull, the slow, irreversible process of breaking a steel-hulled ship went undetected. It was only a matter of time.

COMPANY POLICY – The loss of the *Ulysses* was eventually put down to 'navigational error', though fault was never fully established. Whether Captain Bremner had made a mistake, either by setting a wrong course or by issuing wrong instructions, is not known. One factor that may have played a part in his subsequent thinking, however, was an instruction by the ship's owners to make certain all cargoes reached their allotted destinations, on time and intact.

The Ocean Steamship Company had selected heroes from Greek mythology for naming their ships. After a period of successful trading with ships named *Achilles*, *Ajax* and *Hector*, the company expanded and ordered five new sister ships of approximately 2,000 tons each. These were built between 1869 and 1871, with the *Priam* being constructed by Scott and Co. and the *Hector*, *Menelaus*, *Sarpedon* and *Ulysses* by Leslie and Co. of Newcastle-upon-Tyne.

Just as the company had spent all this money however, they went through a period when their ships were quite clearly not as invincible as their names suggested; something which brought them to the brink of ruin. Between October 1875 and March 1876, the *Hector*, *Orestes* and *Sarpedon* were all lost. These losses, in terms of cargo and vessels, amounted to well over a quarter of a million pounds and was quite disastrous. Nevertheless, this might all have been managed had the rest of the fleet avoided further mishap. When cargo after cargo was lost through a succession of groundings, collisions and breakdowns, the company suddenly found itself in a serious financial predicament of having to find additional funds for repairs and replacement ships at a time of falling income. During her first year afloat, the *Ulysses* went ashore in the Red Sea and was so badly damaged that she had to return to England for

There is plenty of room to enter the wreck and swim between two deck levels.

extensive repairs resulting in a heavy financial loss from that particular voyage. Then came a succession of broken shafts, with three ships having to be docked for repairs. It was at this time that *Ulysses* was very nearly lost altogether when she ran aground near Singapore. After the *Teucer* was lost in 1885, however, this epidemic of misfortune seemed to have passed whereupon every captain was made aware of the policy which required them to deliver their entire cargo in good order and in the most reasonable time.

Meanwhile, unseen, the damage to the *Ulysses* steadily increased as the ship continued to be pounded by a moderate sea. By the morning of 19 August, she was down by the stern. The following day, two lighters, with labourers, arrived from Suez and shortly afterwards HMS *Falcon* also arrived to offer protection. Realising the seriousness of the condition of the *Ulysses*, the captain of the *Falcon* lent some of his crew to assist with unloading, whilst others were landed to guard that which had been jettisoned. It was a long, dirty and laborious task in the most testing of conditions, made even worse by the intense heat which predominates in August. With the engines engulfed and the pumps silenced, foul water was now deep in the holds. The workers had to wade deep into this unpleasantness, at least up to their armpits and at times had to swim underneath. Without power they had to haul the cargo by hand out of the hold and into the sea, where it was man-handled over coral reefs to the shore before finally being carried one third of a mile to the lighters.

Throughout these many days of toil, two other passing ships belonging to the Ocean Steamship Company, hove to and offered assistance. By now, however, the *Ulysses* was beyond saving. Eventually, Captain Bremner could do nothing more than watch as his ship settled down the reef – in an almost leisurely fashion, with her bows and bowsprit still in view, pointing upwards at a sharp angle.

Satisfied nothing more could be done, on 6 September 1887 all parties returned to Suez. The lighters were so fully laden that additional space had to be found on the decks of HMS *Falcon* for a considerable amount of salvaged cargo. On arrival, Bremner made his official report on the loss of his ship and the *Ulysses* was officially listed as 'Abandoned'. Bad weather then set in during which the crippled ship sustained considerable damage before finally disappearing below the surface forever. No specific date for the final sinking was ever recorded.

The *Ulysses*'s cargo was described as 'general merchandise', a term used to describe any consignment of various commodities. Whilst the manifest no longer exists, the resultant court hearing placed a value of £60,000 on that cargo (a vast amount in those days) and specifically mentioned quicksilver (Mercury). A few remnants of cargo are still found inside the ship to this day.

DIVING THE *ULYSSES* – This ship lies up the reef with her stern at 28m. The front one-third or so has suffered through being so very shallow and is now a debris field of broken bits. One or two large pieces, which look like boilers, have been forced across the nearby lagoon and driven onto the distant sandy shore. The main body of the wreck, however, is now on its port side and provides a very interesting dive. Most of the wooden decking has rotted away revealing a framework of iron girders not dissimilar to that of the *Carnatic*. The stern reveals the beautifully rounded features that were the style of day, as sail began to give way to steam. The rudder and propeller are still in place and combine to provide a most photogenic location. Above the stern a number of original features such as bollards, winches and railings are still found, including a large tiller.

The main structure comprises iron cross members. These continue to provide the strength required to keep those elements of the ship which are in deeper water intact, even after more than one hundred and twenty years underwater. With the wooden decking gone, the main hull is wide open with plenty of natural light penetration allowing the diver to enter and explore the vessel at two levels right down to the bottom. Deep inside the ship at the stern, the diver will find what looks like a small number of barrels and part of the propeller shaft. The barrels are actually the solidified contents (probably flour) with the casings having rotted away.

Working forward from the stern, the diver must eventually exit from the wreck at that point where the ship reveals the beginning of the damage caused by so many years underwater on a shallow coral reef. At this point the rear mast has broken from its mounting and reaches from the wreck down to the seabed where the top has come to rest right next to the broken funnel. Just forward of this, is some evidence of the small wheelhouse that was once located amidships. The bridge was yet to be designed. In the 1880s many a captain still preferred to navigate his vessel from the open decks from where, if nothing else, they could at least see.

From this point forward the vessel is well broken up. Large sections of hull and framework become smaller and smaller until the diver encounters a veritable debris field in very shallow water. The wreck plays host to thousands of Vanikoro sweepers (glassfish) and all the usual reef fishes are also in attendance. Over the years the *Ulysses* has become covered in corals and soft corals which have, through their many years of growth, added a new and wonderful dimension to the wreck. In short, this is a very beautiful dive site.

Until 2001, the main body of the *Ulysses* was still upright and always pointing up the reef. Prevailing currents, coupled with the passage of time, however, finally pushed the vessel hard over onto her port side

Divers are able to explore the *Ulysses* – from within and without.

where she will undoubtedly remain as one of the many truly outstanding dive sites of the Egyptian Red Sea.

POSTSCRIPT – Arthur Wellesley Bremner was born in Liverpool in 1843 and gained his Master's Certificate in 1867, at the early age of twenty-four years. He commanded a number of different vessels from 1880 before being appointed to the *Ulysses* in February 1885. There is no record of Captain Bremner returning to duty at sea after the loss of the *Ulysses* in 1887.

Chapter VIII

ROSALIE MOLLER

(GPS: 27° 39·059N, 33° 46·283E)

THE SHIP – Built in Glasgow by Barclay Curle & Co., this general cargo ship was launched as the *Francis* in January 1910 and went into immediate service with the Booth Shipping Line. She was a smart ship for her day with 4 cargo holds – two forward and two aft of a central bridge deck. Her dimensions were 108.23m x 15m with a draught of 7.38m and a displacement of 3,960 grt. She was powered by a 3-cylinder triple-expansion steam engine which provided 401 hp and a top speed of 10 knots (unladen).

In March 1931 she was sold to the Lancashire-based Moller Line and re-named *Rosalie Moller* – it being the practise of that company to give all their vessels female names followed by the surname Moller. Up to this point, the vessel had plied British and European coastal waters. Messrs Moller, however, had other plans for this gallant little ship and she was soon found operating along the east coast of China, between Shanghai and Tsingtao.

The *Rosalie Moller* as the *Francis* in Hamburg Harbour before 1931 when she was renamed. Her tall funnel survived intact for 60 years until being pulled over by someone intent on removing the copper steam whistle found on the leading edge. (World Ship Society)

THE LOSS OF THE *ROSALIE MOLLER* – During the Second World War, the Ministry of Transport laid claim to all vessels that were either British-owned or registered. In the National Maritime Museum, the list of merchant seamen who went down with their ships runs to three large volumes. There were Atlantic convoys, Mediterranean convoys and the dreaded PQ convoys to Murmansk. Some of these were so brutally slaughtered that only one or two vessels survived. Altogether, hundreds of ships went to the seabed and, in so doing, a far greater proportion of Merchant Seamen lost their lives than in any of the Armed Forces.

Some of the older vessels, however, were spared such duties, largely because they were too slow and could not keep up. These were the mighty 'little ships' – left to fly the flag in home waters, doing what they could to keep British trade from grinding to a halt. Nevertheless, they were always available for the war effort, should the need arise.

By the late 1930s war in Europe was looming and the more it became inevitable, the more people had to consolidate their financial positions. The Moller Line was only too aware that if war was declared they would probably never see many of their ships again and 'Loss or Damage due to War Causes' is still an exclusion clause on almost all insurance policies. The options, therefore, were simple; either they recalled their ships and stood by, ready to assist the country at this time of great need, or they risked financial ruin by losing everything.

Consequently, by 1940, the *Rosalie Moller* was back in Liverpool under the proud command of Captain James Byrne, a very experienced master mariner. Byrne was a rather loud Australian whose trademark was his bush hat. He was also a man who ran a tight ship. At thirty years old, the *Rosalie Moller* was an ageing vessel by any standards and her chief engineer spent all his time nursing her engines from crisis to crisis in order to get the very best from them. By now her top speed was only seven knots. Nevertheless, she was ideal for collier duties and was soon making a significant contribution, transporting anything up to 4,500 tons of best Welsh coal to whichever port the Royal Navy demanded. Ever since the advent of steam-driven warships, the Royal Navy had prized the value of 'Best Welsh.' It was an established fact that best Welsh coal burned brighter and made less smoke. The benefits for a navy with coal-fired capital ships was the equivalent of 'more miles per gallon' and less smoke meant that enemy ships were sighted first.

Regularly loading at Cardiff and taking this valuable commodity to any of the Navy's ports from Rosyth to Portsmouth, James Byrne was often seen at the helm of the *Rosalie Moller* with his large wooden pipe clenched firmly in his teeth. He was a hard task-master and whenever he barked, the crew jumped. They all knew, however, if ever they got into a tight spot they would not want anyone else in charge.

The distinctive bows of the *Rosalie Moller*.

Despite her slowness, the time eventually came for the *Rosalie Moller* to venture further afield. The Royal Navy's Force K was operating out of Malta and required re-coaling facilities at both ends of the Mediterranean. With Axis forces occupying most of the north Mediterranean coastline, Malta was under constant siege and whilst warships were generally able to look after themselves, merchant vessels rarely broke through the constant barrage of air and submarine attack. The *Rosalie Moller* had already made a couple of trips to Gibraltar and unloaded her precious cargo at the small dock, known to this day as Coaling Island.

Then, in July 1941, the *Rosalie Moller*'s engines were given a thorough overhaul, before she was assigned the task that would prove to be her last. At the end of that month she loaded 4,680 tons of Best Welsh before saling independently for Alexandria via South Africa. This involved rounding the Cape of Good Hope for the very first time in her thirty-one years afloat. It was a long and uneventful journey and on 11 September she slipped her mooring in Durban and, following another brief stop at Aden, finally entered the Red Sea. On reaching the Gulf of Suez, she was assigned 'Safe Anchorage H' to await further instructions. The master let out the starboard anchor and some 200m of chain allowing the gentle current to push the vessel back. This was good holding ground and, at long last, the engine was closed down. All they could do now was wait.

As explained in Chapter IV, being called forward to proceed through the canal was dependent on several factors; enemy activity, cargo priority and so forth. All this was held up, however, because two vessels had col-

Even at 38m deep, the railings host the most colourful coral growth.

lided further up the Gulf of Suez and were actually blocking the entrance to the entire seaway. This is why the *Thistlegorm*, with her much needed and valuable cargo, remained at anchor for two full weeks before finally becoming lost. It was also the spectacular loss of the *Thistlegorm* in the early hours of 6 October 1941, which lit up the night sky to reveal even more ships at anchor to those retreating German aircraft. Thus it was, on the night of 7 October 1941, Captain Byrne and the crew of the *Rosalie Moller* were blissfully unaware that, at approximately 22.58 hrs, two more twin-engined Heinkels had crossed the north Egyptian coast and were heading South East – straight towards them.

Byrne had a bunk next to the bridge and, awoken by the noise of aircraft engines, stepped outside. Unarmed and unable to defend his ship, the master of the *Rosalie Moller* could only watch as one of the aircraft came in for a low-level attack. Characteristically, he shook his clenched fist in a last gesture of defiance as the aircraft passed close above him and unleashed its deadly cargo. He was later reported in the official War Diary as stating: 'Two bombs released, one striking No. 3 Hold at 00.45 hrs. Vessel sank 01.40 hrs 8 October 1941, two Crew missing.'

Taken from that same War Diary – now declassified, on 10 October 1941, the Admiralty sent a secret message to Washington with regard to salvage. The message commenced:

(1) Following ships now lying sunk Red Sea and on adjacent NE African Coast. In Gulf of Suez and straits of Jubal (sic) *THISTLEGORM* (4,898 tons bombed badly damaged)..... *ROSALIE MOLLER* (3,963 tons bombed)....

So it was that the *Rosalie Moller* was lost almost exactly forty-eight hours after the *Thistlegorm* – with the combined loss of eleven lives. Interest in the *Rosalie Moller*, however, then almost disappeared altogether for one very good reason. After the war, raw materials were in short supply. Throughout the Gulf of Suez many lost ships were raised and salvaged whilst others were cleared as hazards to shipping. Understandably, many of these were wrongly identified by those who had other priorities at the time. At least two separate and independent accounts of the *Rosalie Moller* both record this ship as having been 'raised and broken up after the war' – though, of course, she never was.

DIVING THE *ROSALIE MOLLER* – Today, the *Rosalie Moller* stands as a magnificent example of British engineering. She sits upright on the seabed on an almost perfectly even keel. One of the first things we saw as we approached the wreck was the forward mast, still with the masthead lamp in place at 17m. Below this, the foc'sle is at 39m. The star-

board anchor is deployed with the chain running down to the seabed at 50m and then out of sight. The port anchor remains fully retracted. The railings are largely still in place, as are windlasses, winches, hawsers and other paraphernalia.

Almost eerily somehow, everything still appears to be tidy. Clearly Captain Byrne did run a tight ship and if he was to have lost his vessel under such circumstances, he would have been happy with how she looks

Just below the crosstrees on the foremast of the *Rosalie Moller*, the diver will find a rather substantial Crow's Nest – beneath which are the remains of the access ladder.

For many divers, the first sight of the *Rosalie Moller* is the top of
the foremast at 17m complete with masthead lamp still in place.

today. The cargo hatches have gone – revealing a full cargo of best Welsh
Coal still in place but nothing else seems to be missing. We had, therefore, a high level of expectation as we finally approached the bridge.
When we got there, however, the cupboard was bare. Whilst we can all
accept how the wooden upper decks will have rotted away, it was great to
see all the portholes still in place and not a broken glass anywhere. The
bell, telegraphs, compass and binnacle were, sadly, all missing and the
captain's safe lies forced open on the floor. Doubtless somebody will say –
yet again! – these were removed for important reasons of research and
identification, but surely we can all read what is written on a bell and
enjoy seeing it in its rightful place at the same time.

The worst possible news, however, is reserved for the ship's funnel. For
over sixty years, right up until early 2001, the *Rosalie Moller*'s tall funnel was still standing immediately aft of the bridge albeit with a slight list
to port since the vessel sank. Unfortunately, this magnificent feature
became a victim of the most barbaric form of combined greed and vandalism it has ever been my misfortune to witness during my diving career.
On the leading edge of the funnel was a ladder which led up to a small
platform surrounded by railings. This was the means of access to a magnificent copper steam whistle which had been there ever since the ship
was built in 1910. Now the funnel lies across the decks and over the port
side of the ship. At first I thought some errant skipper had moored his
boat to the funnel and accidentally pulled it over, but not so. On careful
examination, I discovered the whistle was gone and the rivets which had

held it in place, were all torn violently outwards. Clearly, this would have
taken some force and it was quite obvious to me that a boat had been
deliberately tied to that steam whistle in order to pull it free. In so doing,
a great deal of damage was caused to the wreck as trophy hunting
reached an all-time low. For me, this was an act of wanton vandalism!

Moving on, immediately aft of the base of the funnel is the entrance
down to the engine room. Here the diver will find a perfectly preserved
example of an early 20th Century triple-expansion steam engine. Access
is relatively easy and well-lit – but the silt can be disturbed very quickly
and spoil everything. Above decks, the rear mast is also intact as far as
the cross-trees and all lifeboats davits are swung out. In the rear accommodation block, pots and pans still hang in the galley where they are now
concreted to the walls above the large stove.

The decks at the stern are at 35m and below these the rudder is at
45m and hard over to starboard. Curiously, one of the four propeller
blades is missing. There is external damage to both rear quarters – being
slightly more extensive to starboard. This is the damage caused by the
bombs on that fateful night in 1941. The damage is easily missed and
none of the cargo of coal was lost.

The *Rosalie Moller* is not on many of the regular diving routes and
does not enjoy the high levels of underwater visibility one expects from
the Red Sea – 15-20m being maximum. That said, corals are growing
on the decks and the fish life can only be described as prolific. Jacks and
Tuna are always found feeding on the large shoals that congregate in the
mornings. After which, it's the turn of some very large Grouper.

The port side of the bows of the *Rosalie Moller* are easily compared with the
detail shown in the only known photograph of the original ship and act,
therefore, as a splendid aid in confirming the identity of this ship.

The fish life found throughout the *Rosalie Moller* really has to be seen to be believed. This shoal of bigeye were found below the ship's mainmast.

COMMENT – The *Rosalie Moller* is a finely preserved time-capsule from another age of shipping. She is both upright and intact and, all things considered, is a significant addition to Egypt's excellent collection of ship-wrecks. On numerous occasions I have heard divers express a preference for this wreck over the *Thistlegorm*. She is, however, a deep dive and all the necessary care, training and experience must be considered before visiting her. That said, she really is worth the wait and will not disappoint.

POSTSCRIPT – James Michael Byrne was born in Sydney in 1889 and went on to gain his Master's Certificate in Australia in 1924. He was widely regarded as a very competent and all-round first class master mariner. Prior to assuming command of the *Rosalie Moller* he worked extensively in the Far East and came to Britain during the early war years in answer to a call for help with the war effort. After the loss of the *Rosalie Moller*, there are no further entries in the 'British' Register of Ship's Captains against his name. This would suggest that either he never went to sea again or, as is more likely in his case, he returned to his native Australia to continue the fight from there.

Chapter IX

KIMON M

(GPS: 27° 54·803N, 33° 55·913E)

THE SHIP – Built by Kieler Howaldtswerke AG of Kiel, the *Kimon M* was launched as the *Brunsbüttel* in 1952. In later years, as she passed through successive owners, she was renamed *Ciudad de Cucuta* in 1953, *Angela* in 1964 and *Kimon* in 1971. The addition of the post-nominal letter 'M' came in 1975 when she was purchased by her last owners, the Ianissos Shipping Company of Panama.

According to the original specifications, the *Brunsbüttel* was a refrigerated cargo vessel with additional accommodation for twelve passengers. She had 4 cargo holds – two forward and two aft of a central bridge deck. Her dimensions were 121m x 15.8m with a draught of 6.1m and a displacement of 3,129 grt. Below decks she was fitted with an 8-cylinder Howaldt-MAN-Diesel engine. According to Lloyd's Register of Shipping 1977-8, however, the dimensions for the *Kimon M* were slightly less and her machinery was now a 4-stroke, single action 8-cylinder diesel engine built by Waggon & Masch which provided 2,940 hp and a top speed of 12 knots. This is a clear indication of certain structural and machinery

The *Kimon M* under her original name *Brunsbüttel*. Launched in 1952, she was renamed the following year and then had two more names before finally becoming the *Kimon M* in 1975. This is, therefore, a very early photograph of the ship. (World Ship Society)

changes to this ship during her lifetime. The *Kimon M* was widely regarded as a sturdy ship with good sea-keeping qualities.

THE LOSS OF THE *KIMON M* – Whilst I was able to discover a full account of the loss of this ship, the names of the Captain and crew had been listed on page one, which was missing! In December 1978, the *Kimon M* was in the small Turkish port of Iskenderun at the extreme north east corner of the Mediterranean Sea. Her Captain was personally supervising the loading of 4,500 tons of bagged lentils. He was required to keep to a tight schedule and knew the Turkish dockers were always in need of direct supervision. Loading here was always a long, laborious and dusty task, none of which was helped by the searing heat and the need to interpret everything that was said.

Finally the hatches were battened down and made ready for the long journey to Bombay. Only minimal tides exist in this corner of the Mediterranean so, just as soon as the ship was ready and the paperwork completed, the pilot was able to come on board and navigate the ship out of the port. Iskenderun is on the shores of a large bay, opening directly into the Mediterranean and, no sooner had the pilot arrived on board and cast off, it seemed that his task was over and he was already departing. The captain, took only sufficient time to check and confirm his course of SSW, before retiring to his cabin.

It took just over two days for the *Kimon M* to cover the four hundred miles to Port Said where the captain was once again on hand to deal with the authorities. Then the two-hundred mile Suez Canal had to be safely negotiated after which he would face the narrow confines of the more hazardous upper reaches of the Straits of Suez. Day after day he remained on the bridge – drinking copious amounts of coffee in order to stay awake, as he gave his personal attention to every detail of navigating his vessel safely. Then, as the ship approached the wider and, therefore, less hazardous Straits of Gobal, he saw the Sinai begin to fall away to the east and the Egyptian mainland, even further away to the west. Satisfied the dangerous waters had been safely negotiated, he duly handed over control of his ship to his first mate leaving verbal instructions that the course set was not to be altered and that he was to be called in 3 hours. With that he retired to his cabin.

From here it would be several days before the ship left the Red Sea and entered the Indian Ocean and, for the time being at least, he could sleep. It was not long, however, before he was very rudely awoken by an event that may have led to the end of his career. With the engines set at 'Full Speed Ahead' the *Kimon M* had driven hard on to the north east corner of Sha'ab Abu Nuhas Reef. The date was 12 December 1978. The passing cargo ship *Interasja* immediately responded to the *Kimon M*'s distress

The *Kimon M* was not built to withstand the pressures created by resting at such an angle and consequently must be considered unsafe to enter.

The unmistakeable ribbed rudder and propeller of the *Kimon M* – which are not likely to be confused with similar features on other shipwrecks.

call, rescued the entire crew and delivered them safely to Suez two days later.

Lloyd's List dated 13 December 1978, carried the following item:

Casualty Report:

KIMON M. (Panamanian). Port Said Dec 12 – MV *Kimon M*, Iskenderun for Bombay with 4,500 tons of lentils, reported stranded near Safaga, exact position still to be ascertained. All crew reportedly abandoned vessel and rescued by MV *Interasja*, arriving Suez Dec 13-14. (*Kimon M* had passed Suez Dec. 10.).

Lloyd's List dated 14 December 1978, updated that information as follows:

KIMON M. (Panamanian). London, Dec 12 – *Kimon M* struck wreck in position lat. 27 35N, long. 33 55 E. Strait of Gubal (sic). Vessel requires tug assistance on Lloyd's open form (See issue of Dec 13.).

It is not known which wreck the *Kimon M* claims to have hit prior to grounding. This was almost three years before the *Chrisoula K* would go aground, but other ships are known to have grounded here and then been successfully refloated. Perhaps one such grounded vessel gave the impression of being in deep water and the *Kimon M* simply meant to go around her? It does happen. Most important of all, however, is the position given by Lloyd's is exactly where the *Kimon M* is found today.

The initial impact drove the *Kimon M* hard on to the top of the reef, where she stayed for some days. Part of the cargo was recovered during that time but that which was contaminated with seawater was abandoned. Initial surveys reported the damage to the hull to be so extensive she was abandoned as a constructive total loss. With her bows still high up on the reef, prevailing winds and currents began to push the ship hard over onto her starboard side. Throughout this time, the front part of the ship – all the way back to No. 2 Hold, was eventually reduced to scrap metal as the remainder fell back into the deeper water at the base of the reef – still on its starboard side. The one final indignity to befall the *Kimon M* was the salvage of the main engine by means of cutting a large hole through the uppermost port side.

BUT IS THIS THE *KIMON M*? – Considerable confusion has occurred with regard to the correct identification of some of the wrecks on Sha'ab Abu Nuhas Reef. Seasoned travellers to the north Egyptian Red Sea will be familiar with four great shipwrecks which lie across its northern shores, but many havedeparted with the wrong name in their diving log-

The incredible view forward through the remains of No. 2 Hold – with divers and the adjacent reef in the background. This feature provides the diver with the most excellent swim-through.

book. The western-most of these four wrecks is the *Giannis D.* Moving in an easterly direction, the next wreck is the *Carnatic*, followed by the *Chrisoula K* and finally the *Kimon M* – a ship which is continually wrongly described as either the *Olden* or *Seastar* and is also continually confused with the *Chrisoula K.* See following chapter for a fuller explanation and an unravelling of all this confusion.

DIVING THE *KIMON M* – Rough seas and strong currents have reduced the bows to a scattered collection of metal pieces, largely indistinguishable from each other. The main bulk of the wreck, however, is an exciting and rewarding dive. Firstly, though, a word of caution. No ship was ever built to withstand the pressures of its own weight when lying on its side and having now spent over twenty-five years on her starboard side, the *Kimon M* has begun to deteriorate quite noticeably. Bulkheads are collapsing and there are large steel plates which rise and fall with the swell. She must, therefore, be regarded as dangerous. Whilst entry is not recommended, I shall describe the ship, both inside and out.

When we first saw the *Kimon M*, it was as if she had been cut straight across the middle of No. 2 Hold, with nothing apart from scattered debris existing forward of that cut. The bulkhead between the engine room and No. 2 Hold was also removed, creating one of the most exciting underwater scenes I have ever witnessed. Arriving on the wreck above the port side, we dropped into the hole cut by the salver's torch. Looking towards the stern we could see the remains of the engine room, with easy access to all parts. Turning our attention forwards, however, we were looking into a large oblong box with some of my fellow divers in the distance neatly framed against the reef. Between them and us, inside the remnants of No. 2 Hold, were a small number of large Batfish.

Emerging once again, we followed the port side all the way down to the stern where we found a single propeller and a very distinctive ribbed rudder. This is the deepest part of the wreck where the seabed is at 32m. From here we made our way around a very pointed stern to the rear decks where we could either penetrate the rear accommodation or remain outside the wreck and fully investigate the external features. Being the least damaged, most of the stern remains intact – complete with bollards, capstans and railings. The decks themselves are vertical and well colonised by small outcrops of coral and all the usual reef fishes. In between Nos 3 and 4 Holds the main-mast lies parallel to the seabed. One of the large cargo booms completely defies the laws of gravity and reaches straight upwards to within 6m of the surface.

We then approach the rear of the central bridge deck which allowed access to even more accommodation including the Captain's cabin complete with bath-tub. On the outside there are numerous individual deck

The remains of what can only be the Captain's cabin –
because of the personal bathtub.

features to look at before we find ourselves almost back at the point where the dive commenced.

For me, that view through No. 2 Hold towards the reef will always be my one abiding memory of this wreck. This is closely followed by the engine room itself which, in spite of the engine having been salvaged, still leaves much for the diver to see and explore. There are pressure valves, gate valves, vents, dials and gauges of all sizes on each and every side. In every direction, there are pipes, railings, steel ladders canted over at the wrong angle and metal walk-ways now on their sides – and all combining to add much to the overall experience.

Elsewhere, the vessel has long become a natural extension of the nearby reef. Early in the morning, Tuna and Jacks can be seen darting into shoals of smaller fishes as they feed. In the late afternoon, large Grouper are found doing the same thing. During the intervening hours of daylight many of the more richly coloured reef fishes have made the *Kimon M* their home as the vessel slowly continues its transition from man-made object to coral reef.

When first I visited this shipwreck, she was an excellent dive. Sadly, however, she is deteriorating at a very fast pace. A ship can only withstand its own weight provided it remains in an upright position. This is why the *Thistlegorm* and *Rosalie Moller* have both fared reasonably well during their years underwater. In much less time, however, the *Kimon M*

has begun to collapse simply because the load-bearing frames cannot support a hull resting on its side. Consequently, entering this shipwreck must be viewed as particularly dangerous.

POSTSCRIPT – I am informed a Greek tribunal later adjudged the Master of the *Kimon M* as being wholly responsible for the loss of the ship by reason of setting a course which took the vessel directly onto Sha'ab Abu Nuhas Reef before retiring to his cabin. Consequently, his Master's ticket was withdrawn for an indefinite period and he was reduced to the status of First Officer in the process. Whilst worded differently, the Greek system for disciplinary action was very probably similar to the British system at that time. Unfortunately, in the absence of all the crew's names, it has been impossible to confirm what then happened to the Master of the *Kimon M*.

Although much was salvaged, the engine room of the *Kimon M*
still provides the diver with plenty to explore.

Chapter X

CHRISOULA K

(GPS: 27° 54·885N, 33° 55·916E)

THE SHIP – The *Chrisoula K* was built in the German Baltic port of Lübeck by Orenstein-Koppel & Lübecker Maschinenbau AG and launched as the *Dora Oldendorff* in 1954. In 1970 she was renamed *Anna B* and in 1979 finally became *Chrisoula K* on being purchased by the Clarion Marine Company of Piraeus. The original specifications show the *Dora Oldendorff* as a general cargo vessel with 5 cargo holds and a central bridge deck. Her dimensions were 98m x 14.8m with a draught of 6.17m and a displacement of 3,807 grt. She was powered by a 2-stroke single action 9-cylinder diesel engine built by Masch, Augsburg-Nuernberg (MAN AG) which delivered 2,700 hp and a top speed of 12 knots. A comparison with the Lloyd's Register of Shipping for 1981 under the name *Chrisoula K* reveals very little of the vessel had been altered during her twenty-seven years afloat.

It should be noted that the *Kimon M* and *Chrisoula K* were of similar size, both were built in Germany and launched within two years of each

The *Chrisoula K* undergoing sea trials in 1954 prior to being accepted by her new owners as the *Dora Oldendorff*. She was later re-named *Anna B* before finally becoming the *Chrisoula K* in 1979. (Reederei Oldendorff)

other. They eventually suffered the same fate in the Egyptian Red Sea within three years of each other and are now found only a short distance apart.

THE LOSS OF THE *CHRISOULA K* – In August 1981, Captain Theodoros Kanellis was in Italy busily supervising the loading of the Greek registered cargo freighter *Chrisoula K*, which had been assigned a cargo of large patio-type floor tiles to be delivered to Jeddah. It was late in the day by the time the crew secured the last hatch cover for sea, so it was not until first light that the mooring lines were slipped and the ship headed out into the open reaches of the Mediterranean.

It was a long, uneventful journey to Port Said where, as is always the case, the Captain was much in demand as he satisfied the requirements of various port authorities. There then followed the lengthy trip through the Suez Canal followed by the difficult and often treacherous upper reaches of the Straits of Suez. This is another story very similar to that of the *Kimon M* whereby the master insisted on doing everything himself. Not once did he confer with any of his officers and not once did he ask

There is no doubt that the features on the stern of the *Chrisoula K* shown in this photograph match those same features shown in photographs of the original ship. (Deborah Phillips)

any of those officers to check any bearings or calculations made. Hour after hour became day after day and there is only so much the human body is able to withstand before tiredness takes its toll.

So once again, we have a tired master in charge of a ship approaching the Straits of Gobal at the very end of the Gulf of Suez. This is where the sea lanes begin to get wider and – were it not for the presence of Sha'ab Abu Nuhas Reef, any ship could be navigated almost blindfold. Like others before him (and since!) this ship's master relaxed just a little too soon. Entirely satisfied the dangerous waters were now behind his ship, Captain Kanellis set a course which he gave to the officer on watch. That course was also recorded in the ship's log. Only now did this otherwise competent, extremely able and vastly experienced master mariner retire to his cabin. He would have barely closed his eyes before being rudely awoken by the impact of ship on reef.

It was 31 August 1981 and, with her engines set at 'Full Speed Ahead,' the *Chrisoula K* had driven hard onto the north-east corner of Sha'ab Abu Nuhas Reef. Thankfully, her crew survived without injury. Lloyd's List dated 1 September 1981, carried the following item:

CASUALTY REPORT: – *Chrisoula K* (Greek). Suez, Aug 31 – Mv *Chrisoula K* ran aground yesterday in the Red Sea, sustaining serious damage but there were no casualties, shipping sources said today. The vessel hit coral

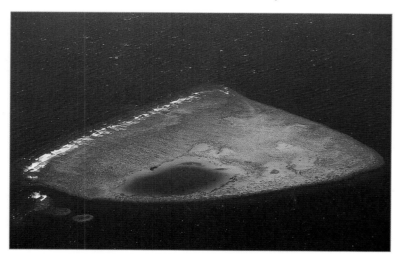

Sha'ab Abu Nuhas Reef from the air. Despite persistent rumours to the contrary, only four major shipwrecks are known to have been lost on this treacherous reef. Those shipwrecks are; *Kimon M,* *Chrisoula K, Carnatic* and *Giannis D.* (Lawson Wood)

reefs near the Egyptian naval base at Râs Banas, about 500 miles south of here, sources at the Assiut Shipping Agency, representing the ship owners, said. Rescue units from the naval base picked up the 21-member crew unscathed and took them to Suez, the sources said. The vessel, carrying a consignment of tiles from Italy, was on her way to Jeddah. The sources said the seriously damaged vessel was considered a total loss. – United Press International.

BUT IS THIS THE *CHRISOULA K*? – Over the years I have read several published reports in which the *Chrisoula K* has been confused with the *Kimon M, Seastar* and *Olden.* As already mentioned, the *Chrisoula K* and *Kimon M* lie a short distance apart and many leading accounts have shown photographs of the one whilst describing the other. Because of the similarities between the two ships, it was, perhaps, inevitable this would happen. As far as the fictitious *Seastar* is concerned, I can find no evidence whatsoever to support the contention that any ship called *Seastar* was ever lost in the Red Sea.

The confusion with the *Olden,* however, is much easier to understand. Having been launched as the *Dora Oldendorff,* the letters 'Olden' were, at one time, still visible on the hull of the *Chrisoula K.* Some insisted, therefore, she was the 'Olden' especially when it became known that a vessel of that name was also lost. For the record, the *Olden* (coincidentally, same original owners as the *Chrisoula K* when she was called *Harmen Oldendorff*) was a 27,288 tonne bulk carrier. Loaded with barley, she cleared Suez on 31 January 1987 and, after striking a reef, later sank in position GPS 27° 31·2N, 34° 17·1E. As anyone armed with the correct chart will observe, this very large ship (much larger than anything found on Sha'ab Abu Nuhas Reef!) now resides in over 1000m of water some 14 miles (22 km) east of Shadwan Island!

Another factor is also quite intriguing. With their true names being unimportant and often not known, local Egyptian seafarers and fishermen have developed their own excellent way of identifying each wrecked ship amongst themselves. They simply call each vessel by the cargo it was carrying. Thus, the *Giannis D* became the Wood Wreck on account of her cargo of sawn timber, the *Carnatic* the Wine Wreck after various bottles were recovered, the *Chrisoula K* the Tile Wreck and the *Kimon M* the Lentil Wreck. Confusing? Not really. At least not until one reads a so-called authentic published account of the SS *Lentil* – a vessel which, like the *Sarah H,* never existed.

Soon after being driven hard onto the reef, the stern of the *Chrisoula K* filled with water and she settled back, leaving the foc'sle high and dry and giving the impression of being entirely separate from the main body of the ship. Naturally, this part of the wreck then suffered at the hands of nature and, over time, the top of the bows, including the foc'sle were reduced to scrap metal. Yes, there is a large triangular piece of metal still found on top of the reef – and many continue to insists this is from the *Chrisoula K*. That wreckage, however, is very likely to be from the *Kimon M*. For sitting right on top of the reef in water barely a metre deep, the diver will find the lower part of the stem – that part which cuts through the water, complete with hawse pipes – which still have their respective anchor chains running through them. Conclusive proof as to the true identity of the wreck is also found elsewhere.

In September 2002, I received a number of photographs from the Oldendorff family archives. They were taken in 1954 and show the *Chrisoula K* on the day she was taken into service as the *Dora Oldendorff*. Two of these photographs show the letters EO emblazoned on her funnel. They stand for Egon Oldendorff, the founder of the company. Although painted over many times in the years after her first name change, these large letters were made of steel plate attached to the funnel's surface. They were never removed. Today, that funnel lies on the seabed off the wreck's starboard side and the 'EO' logo may be found by any diver who cares to make a thorough examination of that funnel's surface. If any further proof were needed, other elements of the ship displayed in those original photographs are easily compared to any number of specific features found underwater.

There is no doubt that these are the bows of the *Chrisoula K*. Photographs similar to this have previously led to speculation that the bows seen here are completely detached from the remainder of the ship. Taken shortly after the *Chrisoula K* was lost in August 1981. (Lawson Wood)

My good friend Shane Brown (who spent almost his entire holiday carrying my spare camera) passes in front of the bridge deck of the *Chrisoula K*. In the background, the decks above Nos 1 and 2 Holds have been reduced by storms and wave action to reveal the ship's 'tween decks.

The *Chrisoula K*'s mainmast still defies gravity and is found
lying parallel to the seabed at a depth of 12m.

All that remains of the bows of the *Chrisoula K* today are found in
very shallow water (1m!) on top of Sha'ab Abu Nuhas Reef.

DIVING THE *CHRISOULA K* – As already mentioned, what remains of the stem is found in very shallow water at the top of the reef. The hawse pipes, with their respective anchor chains still running through them, are dislodged from the wreck and lie alongside. Heading aft, the main body of the wreck is upright with masts and booms having fallen over the starboard side. No. 1 and No. 2 Holds are wide open with their cargo of tiles still in place. Curiously, the decks in front of the central bridge deck, however, have been reduced to tween deck level by a combination of successive winter storms and their relatively shallow disposition.

What remains of the bridge deck has also been battered over the years. Nevertheless, there are several rooms to be explored although, sadly, all were stripped bare a long time ago. There are two entirely separate access points leading down to the engine room, although one of these was obstructed to a point I considered dangerous. Having said that, the engine room is a fascinating place with a profusion of pipes and railings stretching in very direction. Once again, there are all the different sorts of valves, vents, dials and gauges on each and every side. Steel ladders and metal walk-ways all add to the experience and few fish venture here.

Immediately aft of the bridge, the ship has suffered considerable damage with the hull being literally twisted through ninety degrees from upright position to one where the stern lies on its starboard side. This creates an interesting element to the dive where the rear decks and accommodation block suddenly become vertical. Everything here is covered in little outcrops of coral. Despite being on its side, the stern

Large 'patio' type floor tiles litter the entire wreck. Note the *Made in Italy* (in English!) inscription on the upturned tile at bottom right of picture.

remains the least damaged. All the usual bollards, capstans and railings are intact. From the vertical decks, the rear mast is still attached, stretching away from the wreck parallel to the seabed and providing yet another example of a very heavy man-made object continuing to defy the inevitable laws of deterioration and gravity as it adds another dimension to a fascinating scene.

The propeller and rudder are the deepest part of the ship and appear virtually undamaged as they rest on the seabed at 26m. From here, the diver is able to view the entire port side which is now covered in a large assortment of hard corals. With the port side being twisted through those same ninety degrees until it becomes perfectly upright once again, there is a large tear through the steel plates which allows the diver to enter the vessel by a most unconventional route. Entering No. 4 Hold above the untouched cargo of thick patio-type floor tiles, the diver will find most are stamped MADE IN ITALY (yes, in English!) with the majority being still bound together in bundles of twenty. The high levels of damage sustained throughout the wreck's superstructure allow a significant amount of natural light to enter – something which assists divers in their exploration of this very interesting and popular shipwreck.

POSTSCRIPT 1 – Despite various claims that as many as seven shipwrecks may be found on Sha'ab Abu Nuhas Reef, I have yet to either meet or speak with any person who has ever seen more than four. Altogether, there is an abundance of evidence to confirm the fact that those four wrecks are; *Kimon M*, *Chrisoula K*, *Carnatic* and *Giannis D*. Furthermore, I have yet to learn of any other vessel having been permanently lost on this reef. Speculation as to the existence of a fifth wreck may be rife – but that is all it is, pure speculation. In spite of the incontrovertible evidence surrounding the *Chrisoula K* – in terms of the ship, various Lloyd's (and other) reports, historic photographs and her cargo, this has never been enough to satisfy those who refuse to accept simple facts. In a nutshell, I am totally satisfied (and I am not alone in this) that the wreck we have all come to know as the *Chrisoula K* is correctly identified and that any other name applied to this wreck is wrong.

POSTSCRIPT 2 – Whether the Master of the *Chrisoula K* – perhaps through tiredness, made a simple error of navigation, or made another mistake when giving his final instructions to the officer of the watch, or whether it was that officer who made the fateful decision which brought the ship into contact with the infamous Sha'ab Abu Nuhas Reef, is not known. What is known is that today the *Chrisoula K* can be found where she fell and provides all grades of diver with one of the most interesting shipwrecks in Egypt's underwater fleet.

Chapter XI

CARNATIC

(GPS: 27° 54·866N, 33° 55·645E)

THE SHIP – Ordered by the Peninsular & Oriental Steam Navigation Company (long before that marvellous name was reduced to just P&O!) and laid down as the *Mysore*, the name of this ship was changed to *Carnatic* during her construction by Samuda Bros of London. Technically described as an 'iron framed, planked passenger steamer,' she possessed two cargo holds – one fore and one aft. Her dimensions were 89.79m x 11.61m with a draught of 5.64m and a displacement of 2,014 grt. In addition to her square-rigged sails, she was powered by a single 4-cylinder vertical, inverted tandem compound steam engine, also built in London, by Messrs Humphrys and Tennant. This produced a very handsome 2,442 hp and a top speed of 12 knots (13.9 knots during trials). The *Carnatic* was launched in December 1862 and registered by the

The Peninuslar & Oriental Steam Navigation Company's *Carnatic* at Calcutta in 1863. The *Candia* and *Mooltan* belonging to the same company are moored astern. Note the marvellous figurehead. (P&O Archives/QFT Photography)

Peninsular & Oriental Steam Navigation Company in March 1863 before sailing for Calcutta on 27 June. For most of her working life, the *Carnatic* was employed between Suez, Bombay and China and latterly had become the proud command of Captain Philip Jones – one of the ablest officers in the company.

THE LOSS OF THE *CARNATIC* – In August 1869, the steamer *Venetian* was loaded at Liverpool with a general cargo eventually destined for Bombay and in London the *Pera* took on board passengers also heading for that same Indian Port. Within a few days of each other both ships sailed for Alexandria. This was a time when the Suez Canal was nearing completion and due to be opened within three months. Even at this late stage, however, few could have imagined how such a new seaway would change the shape of world trade forever. Up until now, ships had unloaded passengers at Alexandria, from where they endured a two-hundred mile journey overland to Suez before joining another vessel and resuming their voyage. A considerable amount of cargo was also transported in the same way.

The passengers on board the *Pera* enjoyed an uneventful trip to the Straits of Gibraltar and a similarly quiet journey along almost the entire length of the Mediterranean before their ship grounded off Alexandria. Here, they remained for three hours before floating off with the tide. Despite this minor mishap, they were mostly at ease and looking forward to joining the more opulent *Carnatic*, the pride of the fleet. The long trek to Suez was a frightful journey in the most oppressive of conditions, but there really were no alternatives and everyone knew they would soon be enjoying cool evening sea breezes. In the meantime, the masters of both the *Pera* and *Venetian* had played their part and were already heading back to England.

Progress overland was always slow, so it was not until the second week of September that Captain Jones was able to supervise the arrival and stowage of both passengers and cargo. He exercised great care; some of his cargo was very valuable and every single item had to be thoroughly checked, accounted for and secured. Finally, everything was ready and Jones was now in charge of thirty-four passengers, one hundred and seventy-six crew and a cargo of cotton bales, copper sheeting, Royal Mail, and £40,000 in specie (unfinished coin money) destined for the Indian Mint.

At 10.00 hrs on the morning of Sunday 12 September 1869, Captain Jones ordered the mooring lines slipped, and so began the final leg of the journey to Bombay. In the seven years since her launch, both the *Carnatic* and Jones had become veterans of the Suez-India route. His was a sleek ship with proud lines and, unlike many of the hybrid sail-and-steam ships of the period, responded well to either form of power. Jones personally negotiated the long narrow confines of the hazardous Gulf of Suez and remained on the bridge to give his personal attention to every single detail of navigation. Not a man to trust any of his more junior officers, he fully intended to remain on the bridge until they reached the open Red Sea.

Maintaining a steady speed of 8 knots, the revolving light at Ashrafi was sighted at 23.40 hrs and by the time the second mate came on duty just after midnight, this was already three miles astern. The night was clear, with a slight following breeze and a little land haze, common in these parts. More importantly, the headlands and islands through which the *Carnatic* plotted her course, were all visible. At 01.00 hrs, Shadwan Island was sighted by the second mate, bearing dead ahead. This was reported direct to the master who altered course to 'South 46° true and gradually to South 51° true.'

At 01.18 hrs breakers were seen off the starboard bow and the helm was instantly put hard-a-starboard and the engines to full speed astern. It was too late and the *Carnatic* struck Sha'ab Abu Nuhas Reef where she became firmly fixed. Not a man to panic or over-react, Jones was most thorough in checking every single aspect of the ship's condition. As the various reports were received, he was quite satisfied that the pumps could handle the amount of water being taken on and that passengers and crew were as safe as could be expected. He decided, therefore, everyone would

Reproduced from *The Illustrated London News* dated 16 October 1869, this picture shows a contemporary artistic impression of the sinking of the *Carnatic* the previous month. *(The Illustrated London News Picture Library)*

Divers swimming along the wreck of the *Carnatic* heading towards the bows.

A diver investigates the finely moulded stern of the *Carnatic*.

remain on board. Whether or not this decision was influenced by the value of the specie on board has always been a matter of conjecture.

At daybreak Jones assessed the situation once again. It was clear the *Carnatic* was stuck fast on a large coral reef – some three miles from Shadwan Island and, although the ship was leaking, she was still in pretty good shape and the pumps were coping. In a bid to lighten the vessel in the hope she might float off the reef, Jones ordered a large proportion of the cotton dumped overboard. Whilst there was no panic amongst the passengers, some did make it known that they wanted to take to the lifeboats and head for the comparative safety of Shadwan Island. The master, however, would hear none of it and insisted that life continued much as before on the stricken ship.

At first sight, this might appear somewhat reckless but Jones was well aware of the dangers involved in moving 210 people in small boats to a remote island three miles from the far side of a dangerous coral reef. He also knew of the deprivations they would suffer until rescued. For the moment at least, his ship was sound and they had power and considerable comfort. Jones also knew that the company's passenger steamer *Sumatra* was due to pass by at any time, inbound for Suez and he fully expected to be rescued later that day. In the meantime, extra lookout was kept for any passing ship.

Of course, none came and, as evening fell, a deputation of passengers approached the captain again with a plea to be allowed to reach Shadwan Island by lifeboat. Once again, they were denied. Totally underestimating the power of a coral reef to 'work' his ship and inflict damage on a steel hull, Captain Jones made the fatal decision to spend another night on board. Accepting both his wisdom and his authority, the passengers dressed for dinner, the waiters served drinks, a sumptuous evening meal was enjoyed by all and afterwards, some of the passengers strolled along the decks almost as though nothing were amiss. For some, however, it would prove to be their last meal.

As the *Carnatic* gently pivoted on top of the coral head that held her so firmly in place, the leaks got worse. What went undetected, however, was the slow, irreversible process which was weakening the keel as it steadily rocked to and fro. It was only a matter of time. By 02.00 hrs on the morning of the 14th, the level of water within the ship finally engulfed the boilers and the ship lost all power and light. Now even more passengers wanted to leave, but still the master placed his faith in the timely arrival of the *Sumatra*. By daybreak, however, the sea state had increased and water was rapidly filling the ship. Only now did Captain Jones finally accept his ship was lost. He ordered the lifeboats made ready and at 11.00 hrs the first passengers were ordered to disembark.

Tragically, and most violently, it became too late for some. In the time-

My diving partner – Shane Brown, is dwarfed by the
huge propeller of the *Carnatic*.

honoured tradition of women and children first, the only three ladies and one child on board had barely taken their seats in one of the small clinker-built lifeboats when the *Carnatic* suddenly, and without warning, split in two. Thirty-three hours on top of a coral outcrop had proved too much for the gallant ship and, with her back broken, she snapped in two with the aft section sinking immediately. Five passengers and twenty-six crew perished. Instantly much lighter, the fore section fell over onto its port side and began to slip off the reef, spilling almost everyone into the sea as it did so. Then, with all surviving passengers and crew fighting for their very lives amongst masts, spars, rigging and all manner of debris, they were engulfed by the returning wave caused by the sinking stern. If ever there was a call for 'All Hands' this was it and, as the freed lifeboats floated off, there were many instances of bravery and brute strength as passengers and crew forgot their respective positions and worked together for the common purpose of saving themselves and each other.

One by one, the survivors were firstly hauled to safety and then taken to a rallying point where other lifeboats had been placed together in the shallow waters above the reef. Then it was a matter of collecting anything that might be needed and, with a final scan for more survivors, it was time to leave. Shadwan Island, however, was not simply three miles away. It was three miles from the far side of Sha'ab Abu Nuhas Reef. In order to shorten the journey considerably, each of the seven lifeboats was hauled across the shallow waters above the reef by the men taking it in turns to pull. Finally, this small, pitiful flotilla was able to row the remaining distance to Shadwan. It was the longest three mile journey any of them had ever travelled and it was already after sunset when they arrived. Once again, they had to negotiate yet more coral reefs in order to land, but they did so quite safely.

Rescue was now their only thought, but in the meantime they had to survive and here they were rather fortunate. Many of the bales of cotton jettisoned earlier had washed up on the Island and, being so tightly packed, were still very dry inside. They were actually bales of calico, a form of course muslin. Being material, however, they immediately provided rudimentary clothing and warmth for the cold night ahead plus bedding for the ladies. More importantly, however, a large amount was immediately carried to the highest point on the island and set alight. At last the overdue *Sumatra* was sighted and responded immediately to the only signal rocket in their possession. A similar ship to the *Carnatic*, the *Sumatra* hove to and dispatched two boats to investigate. By now, however, it was 9 p.m. and all agreed it was far too dangerous to negotiate the coral reefs at night. It was not until the following morning, therefore, that all survivors were taken safely on board the *Sumatra* which then completed her journey to Suez.

In the 1860s, The Peninsular & Oriental Steam Navigation Company did not insure their vessels against loss. Instead, they covered such eventualities from a special reserve fund. This is why this particular *Carnatic* is not found in Lloyd's Register of Shipping – though there are other ships with the same name. Our *Carnatic*, however, had been the pride of the fleet and her loss plunged the company into serious financial difficulties, with their shares dropping sharply and then falling again as new survivors' accounts were published. In the meantime, Jones faced an official enquiry.

The resultant Board of Trade enquiry described the *Carnatic* as a 'fully equipped and well-found ship' and Captain Jones as 'a skilful and experienced officer.' With respect to the stranding, however, they stated 'it appears there was every condition as regards ship, weather and light to ensure a safe voyage and there was needed only proper care. This was not done, and hence the disaster.'

With Jones seeking to blame an unusually strong current for moving him from his allotted course, the Court stated that the Master should have taken a bearing from Ashrafi Light to ascertain his precise position. The Court's decision was, therefore, that the stranding of the *Carnatic* was 'due to a grave default of the Master' and consequently suspended his Master's Certificate for 9 months from 29 Nov 1869. When it came to the question of the steps taken by the Master for the protection of the passengers and crew after the stranding, the members of the court were unanimous in their opinion 'that when it was determined to leave the ship, the master and his officers in their exertions to secure the safety of the passengers, did all that experienced and brave men could do.'

RECOVERING THE SPECIE – The cargo, however, *was* insured and being of such great value (the equivalent of several million pounds by today's standards), Lloyd's immediately dispatched Captain Henry Grant to take charge of a salvage operation. On arrival in Suez, Grant discovered there was only one diver available to him. He was also wrongly informed the *Carnatic* had sunk in over forty fathoms (more than 70m!) and later admitted he almost turned back. Having come so far, however, he decided the least he could do was take a look and arrived on the scene of the sinking on 29 September. Immediately chasing away some local Arab boats, Grant was heartened to find the *Carnatic* in quite shallow water at the bottom of a reef with some of her features still visible above the surface.

Working from the Egyptian vessel *Tor*, Grant's only diver was Stephen Saffrey from Whitstable (a name still common in that town) but adverse weather conditions delayed his first descent until 15 October. Grant had been informed that, in readiness for an orderly evacuation, Captain Jones had ordered the specie moved to the mail room and this is where the search began. A body was recovered, mailbags were sent to the surface and pocket watches removed from the safe, but no boxes of coins.

Next to the mail room was a post office but entry necessitated the removal of a large internal bulkhead. Working for long hours on his own, this task took Saffrey several days. Finally, he was through and, on the

My diving partner – Dave Shields inside the forward section of the wreck.

24th recovered another 16 mailbags – just in time for them to be handed to a passing steamer and resume their interrupted journey to Bombay. The first box of specie was brought to the surface on the 26th and this was followed by a steady stream of the heavy boxes until the task was completed on 8 November. In the meantime, local Bedouin free divers had recovered over seven hundred sheets of fine-grade copper that was also still destined for India's Mint.

Official reports of the salvage show the entire cargo of specie to have been recovered. Having been found in a very secure and undisturbed part of the ship, no other outcome was ever likely. That said, we all enjoy stories of treasure and the *Carnatic* has spawned one or two of its own such tales – including one of missing gold bullion, over the years. Today, however, the real treasure is found in the vessel's beautiful lines, still a magnificent sight, even after more than a century underwater.

WHO WAS FIRST? – From 1869 the wreck soon became forgotten as successive generations of seafarers came and went. In the early 1980's, however, a new form of tourism - scuba diving tourism, was beginning to take a firm hold in the Egyptian sector of the Red Sea and one of the pioneering liveaboard diving boats was called Lady Jenny V. The wreck of the Carnatic was first discovered by Adrian O'Neil, captain of the Lady Jenny V, in 1985. Lawson Wood was one of the first people to be shown the wreck and set about resolving the question of her identity in his usual professional manner. On 2 February 1987, after much research, he received a letter from P&O confirming the fact that the wreck was indeed the Carnatic and seven days later obtained further confirmatory information from the National Maritime Museum at Greenwich, London. It was, therefore, the combined skills of Adrian O'Neil and Lawson Wood which were responsible for the discovery of this particular shipwreck.

DIVING THE CARNATIC – The *Carnatic* had become a long forgotten part of Egypt's maritime heritage until divers, searching for a much later shipwreck, happened upon her remains. It was then that subsequent research revealed this tragic, yet fascinating, story from another age of both shipping and diving. Many accounts, however, still describe the wreck as being in two separate halves, if only because she did break in two with each half sinking separately. Visiting the wreck, however, will reveal what must be one of the most incredible postscripts to any shipwreck story as those two halves fell to the seabed just as they might have done had they gone down as one piece.

The *Carnatic* lies on her port side, parallel with the base of the reef with her keel towards that reef. Her bows face east and her stern west. Bearing in mind the manner of her sinking, there are three distinct elements to this dive. The fore and aft sections are still largely intact and are joined together by a very badly damaged area – the amidships, where the ship broke and, where the engine room was located. It is a fairly con-

Coral growth on the decks of the *Carnatic*.

stant 25-27m to the seabed and 18-20m to the upper (starboard) side, throughout the dive. The wooden superstructure and planking has almost all disappeared though many fragments are still found. What is revealed is a steel hull held together by iron cross-members allowing the diver to explore down through two deck levels within the wreck itself.

Commencing at the bows, there is a large copper ring that once held the bowsprit in place below which is the ship's leading curved metal bowsprit support. Underneath this was once found the ship's quite marvellous and distinct figurehead – sadly now rotted away to nothing. Looking back along the wreck, even today it is still quite easy to see and appreciate the *Carnatic*'s fine, sleek lines.

From the bows, the ship gently widens to the main body where, on both sides, lifeboat davits are swung out. These are, however, usually missed by divers because the preferred route from stem to stern is to enter the vessel and swim between the two levels of iron framework. This is a fascinating encounter with something built in 1862! On one of my many visits to this wreck, I even found a small brass porthole which I immediately covered with debris in the vain hope it would remain where it was for a while longer. Emerging from this forward section, the diver then encounters the most severely damaged part of the wreck. Whilst some might describe this as nothing more than a pile of scrap metal, it does, nevertheless, still provide plenty of scope for exploration and investigation. After all, that 4-cylinder vertical, inverted tandem compound steam engine is still in there, somewhere.

Below decks in the forward section of the wreck of
the *Carnatic* are the remains of a Capstan

For many, the stern section remains the most exciting and interesting part of the dive. Very similar to the fore part - allowing the diver to swim deep inside. As with the Ulysses, I originally thought I was looking at some old barrels but later realised it was the solidified contents which had retained the barrel shape. Above decks, more lifeboat davits are found swung out on both sides.

The very best aspect of the entire vessel, however, requires the diver to swim right around the stern, away from the wreck and then look back at that stern. My first reaction on seeing this finely moulded example of Victorian craftsmanship with its single row of seven square windows, was that it was so reminiscent of the style of ships' sterns in Nelson's day. It is also easy to begin to understand how traditional styles of shipbuilding had evolved over the many years of building wooden ships and how they were now being adapted for steel. Below those windows, the stern curves gracefully round and inwards as it reaches down towards the magnificent rudder – next to which is that feature which was certainly not found in the time of Nelson; an enormous three-bladed propeller resting on the sand.

After such a long time underwater, it is fairly safe to assume the *Carnatic* is likely to remain pretty much as she is for the foreseeable future. She is well colonised by hard corals, soft corals and her own indigenous population of reef fishes. Altogether, she is probably one of the finest examples of shipwreck from her time found anywhere in the world and is, therefore, well worth a visit. Should you do so, however, spare but a thought for those who lost their lives.

POSTSCRIPT NO. 1– Captain Philip Buton Jones was born in Liverpool in 1830 and gained his Master's Certificate in London in 1858 at the age of twenty-eight years. His commands included the *Columbian*, *Mongolia*, *Surat* and *Syria* before being appointed to the *Carnatic* in 1867. He was also a serving officer in the Royal Navy Reserve and by 1869 had secured a reputation of being one of the ablest master mariners afloat. After the loss of the *Carnatic*, Captain Jones never returned to sea.

POSTSCRIPT NO. 2– I am indebted to Mr Robert Garrett for copying the following inscription found on a white marble tablet in his parish church in Dublin:

> In memory of Ensign Edmund Francis Floyd Cuppage, of the 38th (1st Staffordshire) Regiment; youngest son of the late Edmund Floyd Cuppage, of Clare Grove, Co. Dublin, Esquire; who was lost on the 13th September 1869 by the foundering of the "Carnatic" in the Red Sea, when on his way to join the service companies of the regiment aged 19 years. This tablet has been erected by his brother officers as a token of their regret at his untimely end.

• Chapter XII •

GIANNIS D

(GPS: 27° 34·680N, 33° 55·565E)

THE SHIP – Launched in 1969 as the Shoyo Maru, the *Giannis D* was built by the Kurushima Dock Company of Imabari, Japan. Officially described as a general cargo vessel, she possessed two cargo holds forward of a bridge and engine room located at the stern. Her dimensions were 99.5m x 16m with a draught of 6.53m and a displacement of 2,932 grt. Her engines were built by Akasaka Tekkosho KK of Yaizu, Japan and comprised a 4 stroke, single action, 6 cylinder diesel, capable of producing 3,000 hp and a top speed of 12 knots.

In 1980, however, the ship was sold to the Dumarc Shipping and Trading Corporation of Piraeus, Greece who renamed the vessel *Giannis D* and placed a large capital D onto her funnel – as was their tradition.

In 1975 she was re-named *Markos*. Interestingly, some people have come to refer to this wreck by the misnomer 'Markos D' and false details of other fictitious wrecks called by the derivatives *Markos, Marko, Markus* and even *Marcus* continue to be published from time to time.

THE LOSS OF THE *GIANNIS D* – I was able to obtain an account of the loss of the *Giannis D* from the Dumarc Shipping and Trading Corporation – but the name of the ship's captain was not included.

The *Giannis D.* (FotoFlite)

In April 1983, the *Giannis D* was loaded with a cargo of sawn softwood in the Croatian port of Rijeka – destined for the Saudi Arabian port of Jeddah and Hodeida on the coast of Yemen. It was a clear spring morning as the Captain ordered the mooring lines slipped and the pilot guided the vessel out into the Adriatic before returning to port by pilot launch shortly thereafter. The journey down through the azure-blue waters of the Adriatic and across the Mediterranean Sea was uneventful, with much of the fairly straightforward navigation being left to the officer of the watch.

The Captain had been a master mariner for almost twenty years and had learned his trade in these waters – which he knew as well as any man. He was also well aware that his presence would be much needed just as soon as they approached the Suez Canal and that he would then get precious little rest until they cleared the Straits of Gobal. They made good time to Port Said and, as they approached this very busy port, the Captain was soon back on the bridge in charge of his ship once again.

Like any other country, the Egyptian authorities have a number of routine checks for any vessel entering their territorial waters. With the Arab-Israeli War still ongoing, however, this was a difficult and occasionally volatile time. Those authorities, therefore, had to be satisfied that neither contraband nor weapons were being smuggled either into or through Egypt. For vessels like the *Giannis D*, the many rules and additional checks were both time consuming and tiresome. Only the captain is ultimately responsible for every single aspect of the ship, its crew and contents, so only he could satisfy the many demands put upon him by the different agencies – all of whom wanted to speak to him and nobody else. That said, they were never deliberately obstructive and when the *Giannis D* had satisfied all the various requirements, she was allowed to proceed.

A canal pilot was then taken on board to shepherd the ship from Port Said to Suez and, by working closely with the Captain – who always remains in command of his ship, the *Giannis D* completed yet another safe passage. Once through the canal and into Suez Bay, the *Giannis D* was stopped just long enough to allow the pilot to disembark. For him, it would soon be another ship and a return to Port Said. The *Giannis D*, however, now faced one of the busiest and most testing stretches of water found anywhere in the world.

Like so many others before and after him, this master mariner decided to conduct the navigation of the Gulf of Suez – complete with its small islands, coral reefs, oncoming surface traffic and oil rig platforms, personally. He was a proud man who enjoyed the role of being the *only* person on board who was able to complete this complex task of navigation – although, of course, he wasn't. Foolishly, from the moment they had reached Port Said, he stayed on the bridge day after day and night after night determined to prove a wholly unnecessary point without seeking either help or so much as a second opinion. In so doing, he was not the only ship's captain to have made the mistake of remaining in charge of a ship long after he was unfit through being far too tired.

As we have seen before, only when the ship was approaching the Straits of Gobal and, with it, the wider open aspects of the Red Sea, did this captain finally hand over control to his officer on watch. Once again, therefore, we have a captain who failed to take account of that certain magnificence which barely reaches the surface and, from a distance, is not easily seen at all – that coral plateau called Sha'ab Abu Nuhas Reef.

Like all reefs, Sha'ab Abu Nuhas is at its most dangerous when the sea is flat calm and there are no breaking waves to betray her precise location to unsuspecting mariners. 19 April 1983 was just such a calm day and, whilst there may be radar reflectors and solar-powered lights on top of the reef – and all regularly maintained in difficult conditions, they remain barely visible to the human eye even during daylight. Unfortunately, at least as far as shipping is concerned, Sha'ab Abu Nuhas is the very last obstacle facing vessels outbound from Suez on their way to the open Red Sea. With Jeddah still another six hundred miles further south and believing only the open sea was between him and his first destination, the master retired to his cabin and was soon fast asleep. With her engines set at Full Ahead, the *Giannis D* was seen to suddenly veer from her allotted course and drive hard onto the north-west corner of Sha'ab Abu Nuhas Reef.

The *Giannis D* very soon after she ran aground on Sha'ab Abu Nuhas Reef in April 1983. Note the cargo of sawn softwood is still on the decks. (Lawson Wood)

This photograph looks forward across the cargo holds of the *Giannis D* towards the bows and was taken soon after she was wrecked in April 1983. (Lawson Wood)

Looking straight down the ship's forward mast
towards the bows in the distance.

The upper reaches of the *Giannis D* are very shallow which makes this an
excellent starting place for those who have never visited a shipwreck before.

Lloyd's List dated 22 April 1983, carried the following item:

Casualty Report:
GIANNIS D (Greek). London Apr 21 – Information received, dated Apr
20, states: Mv *Giannis D*, (from Rijeka), cargo sawn softwood for dis-
charge at Jeddah and Hodeida, grounded at Sha'ab Abu Nuhas, approximate position lat. 27 35N, long. 33 56E, last night. Crew abandoned
vessel, which is listing, and taken by an Egyptian tug to Santa Fe platform and then by helicopter to Râs Shoke. Owners signed Lloyd's standard form with salvage tug *Salvanguard*, which proceeding to vessel.

DIVING THE *GIANNIS D* – On first being lost, the *Giannis D* came to
rest on top of the reef with successive waves washing her cargo of wood
from her decks and holds. After some months she then broke and sank
beneath the surface, coming to rest at the base of the reef which had
claimed her. Today, the *Giannis D* is found in three separate sections;
bows, amidships and stern. Whilst each of these will provide the diver
with a most rewarding dive, most prefer the stern which is quite dra-
matic. Such is the power of nature to reduce a man-made object to scrap
metal, that the stern looks as though it has been cleanly cut from the
remainder of the ship by an acetylene torch.

Almost like an island in the sand, it sits proudly all by itself, canted over towards the port side at an angle of about forty-five degrees. Only 23-24m at its deepest point, part of the superstructure reaches to within a few metres of the surface. The propeller is found trapped under the rear starboard quarter, which lies very close to the base of the nearby reef. Over the stern, the ladder used by the crew to abandon ship is still hanging down the side. Swimming around the huge, curved stern, one finds the port companionway touching the sand with a number of davits and other fittings hanging out from the wreck – some of which are touching the seabed. There are Crown-of-thorns starfish here – so watch where you put your hands.

Above the port companionway, the diver will find two raised deck levels; one above the other. Immediately aft of this is the funnel – complete with that large letter 'D.' Below the funnel it is relatively easy to enter the engine room. This was never salvaged and offers a very exciting interlude for those who like to venture inside. As one would expect, all the usual dials, gauges, valves and pipes stretch in every direction. In addition, the steel ladders, railings and metal walk-ways are all now canted over at awkward angles. Most important of all, the engines are intact and offer an exciting opportunity for photography – before the silt becomes disturbed.

Back on the outside, the bridge occupies the leading edge of this stern accommodation. It comprises a large open room with plenty of light and a number of entry and exit points. Being so shallow (6-8m) and well lit,

Looking aft along the port side of the *Giannis D*.

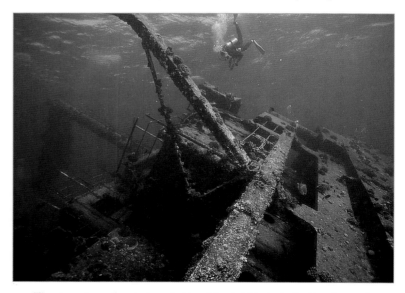

The view above the starboard side of the bridge deck, looking forward.

My diving partner Shane Brown swims forward along the port companionway. Note the 'Crown of Thorns' starfish to his left.

this bridge provides an excellent opportunity for those wishing to enter a shipwreck for the very first time. Immediately in front of the bridge, a number of cargo winches are found on the decks below a very large A-Frame, which was once used for hoisting cargoes. Swimming east, and generally parallel to the reef on the right, the diver passes over the remains of No. 2 Hold before arriving at a raised section which once separated the two cargo holds. Part of the port companionway is uppermost with the mainmast and booms lying across the seabed. Continuing in the same direction, past the remains of No. 1 Hold which lie flat on the seabed, the diver will see a few well-rotted remnants of cargo before arriving at the ship's bows.

This structure is a completely separate dive and often overlooked. The bows rest perfectly on their port side with the vertical decks facing away from the reef. Once again, they look as though they were separated from the remainder of the ship by an acetylene torch. Being exactly on their side, means that the fore-mast is found stretching out directly above and parallel to the sand – yet another example of the defiance of all the laws of gravity. Many hard and soft corals have begun to colonise the mast and numerous fishes have crossed over from the adjacent reef to set up home. On more than one occasion, I have encountered a huge Napoleon Wrasse here which appears to be unafraid of divers. On the decks, are the windlass and a number of cargo winches, all still occupying their rightful

place. There is also a small entrance into the tight confines of the forward anchor locker, but with so much chain still inside, there is nothing to be gained from the experience.

POSTSCRIPT – It has often been suggested that the loss of the *Giannis D* was a deliberate act of wrecking. Having looked at the few facts that are available to me, I do not believe any mariner would deliberately endanger the lives of his fellow crew by driving his ship onto the rocks – at 'Full Speed!' Whether tiredness played a part and a wrong calculation was made or whether the *Giannis D* suffered a critical equipment malfunction to cause her to veer off course was, apparently, never actually determined. I am informed that the resultant enquiry removed the names of captain and crew from their final deliberations in which they stated that tiredness might have been the cause of the ship being off course but that other factors could not be ruled out. In the absence of specific evidence, therefore, no cause was established.

Chapter XIII

MINIYA

(GPS: 27° 13·566N, 33° 50·815E)

THE SHIP – Project 254 was a routine code name for the development and production of minesweepers for the Soviet Navy. The original planning was assigned to a task group in Leningrad which later became the Western Planning & Design Office. Having previously achieved limited success with mine counter measures, this department was tasked to design a new class of ocean minesweeper in 1946. The designs were approved later that same year and only modified for mass production. These new ships were designated T-43 class Ocean Minesweepers. The original ships were then built in Leningrad and Kerch, with the first vessel entering service in 1948. At that time, such ships were quite revolutionary and able to tow a much more modernised sweep, providing the Soviet Navy with an overall sweep capacity of three times that which was previously available. Further enhanced versions of this type of ocean minesweeper continued to be produced for several years, with some of the latter units being built in Poland and even China.

Between 1956 and 1962 Egypt purchased five Soviet type T-43s, and renamed them *Bahaira*, *Charkieh*, *Dakhla*, *Gharbia* and *Miniya*. In 1970, they purchased a further two more (*Assiut* and *Sinai*). Today, the *Sinai* is moored at Hurghada and is almost identical to the *Miniya* found on the seabed a short distance away.

Between 1956 and 1962 Egypt purchased five of these boats which were then renamed *Bahaira* (Ex-301), *Charkieh* (Ex-304), *Dakhla* (Ex-305), *Gharbia* (Ex-306) and *Miniya* (Ex 302). The fate of the first four of these ships is not known but, according to *Conway's All the World's Fighting Ships 1947-1982*, the *Miniya* is recorded as having been sunk in the Gulf of Suez by Israeli aircraft on 6 February 1970. Later that same year the Egyptians purchased two more of this type of ship; the *Assiut* (Ex-303) and *Sinai* (NK). Today, the *Sinai* can still be seen moored at Hurghada.

The Soviet T-43 class Ocean Minesweeper had dimensions of 58m x 8.5m with a draught of 2.4m and a displacement of 569 tons (full load). Below decks the machinery comprised two 4-stroke turbo-charged Type-9D diesel engines which provided 2,200 hp and a top speed of 14 knots – reduced to 8.4 knots with sweep deployed in deep water. Each vessel had a range of 3,800 nautical miles at 10 knots. No information about any changes made to the armaments used on this type of ship is available. Whilst any of the weaponry supplied by the Soviet Union might have been replaced or modified, this is considered unlikely. The original Soviet weapons were: 2 x twin 37mm machine guns, one fore and one aft; 2 x twin 12.7mm machine-guns – mounted immediately in front of the bridge, and any combination of up to sixteen mortars or thirty-nine mines.

GETTING THE NAME RIGHT! – The wreck of the *Miniya* is found inshore not very far from Hurghada Harbour – and not in the Gulf of Suez as previously mentioned. She lies very close to the *Excalibur* – a small charter yacht lost in mysterious circumstances some years ago. Over time, this entire area outside the harbour has become known as 'El Mina' – a name which is a combination of mis-spelling *El Miniya* and the corruption of an Arabic word for 'the harbour' which sounds very like El Mina. Consequently, this minesweeper became wrongly known as *El Mina*.

THE LOSS OF THE *MINIYA* – The third Arab-Israeli War took place over 5-10 June 1967 and became known as the Six-Day War. Israel occupied the Gaza Strip, captured the Golan Heights from Syria, took Old Jerusalem and the West Bank from Jordan and also occupied the Sinai Peninsula as far as Suez. Throughout the six days of conflict, fighting was brief but intense. The fourth Arab-Israeli War took place between 2-14 October 1973 and became known as the Yom Kippur War when Egyptian forces re-crossed the Suez Canal and made significant gains. After the Camp David Agreement in 1978, Israel finally withdrew from the Sinai Peninsula over the period 1979-1982.

According to Conway's, the *Miniya* is recorded as being sunk by Israeli forces on 6 February 1970 but no further details are given and no information about the action itself is available. With her port anchor run out, it would appear the ship was at anchor when she was surprised and sunk by aircraft fire. The vessel sustained a direct hit on the starboard quarter which left a large gaping hole and created a corrugated effect on the starboard side of the bridge deck. It is likely that the force of the explosion blew the forward mounted twin 37mm machine gun overboard before the ship sank.

DIVING THE *MINIYA* – The *Miniya* lies squarely on her port side at a depth of 30m to the seabed. She is close to shore and is marked with a small buoy permanently fixed to her starboard propeller. The vessel is completely intact apart from that forward deck gun which is likely to be found nearby. The best way to tackle this wreck is to follow the line down to the stern and swim all the way to the bows at a depth of about 25m. This allows the diver to follow a line which is roughly along the middle of the decks before swimming all the way back to the stern, above the ship's uppermost starboard side.

Taking this route, the first item encountered is the port propeller which has lost one of its blades. Several bits of old rope are tied to both propeller shafts. Right above the stern is a low platform on which is fitted a device for controlling the wire cables used for minesweeping. Below this, the stern itself received something of a battering at one time. Heading forward, on top of the aft accommodation is one of the 2 x twin 37mm machine guns. The gun is still loaded with live ammunition and appears to have been cleared for action and might even have been in use when the ship sank. The next recognisable feature is the ship's funnel on which there is a small ladder running up the starboard side. In front of the funnel are a number of cable winches firmly secured to the decks. Originally used for the deployment of Paravanes when the vessel was engaged in mine sweeping, each winch has its own wire cable still neatly coiled in place.

On top of the rear of the bridge deck was fitted the radio antennae tower. That tower is now fallen down to the seabed and has become a jumble of scrap metal. Right in front of the bridge are the damaged remains of the 2 x twin 12.7mm machine guns which were mounted, curiously, in such a position as to obscure much of the view from the bridge when in use. Once again these guns are complete, still loaded with live ammunition and also appear to have been cleared for action. The starboard bridge door is wide open. Looking inside, it becomes obvious how conditions on board this type of ship were always very cramped. Now, after more than thirty-five years underwater, much of the interior

The Bridge Deck of the *Miniya* revealing her attitude of hard over onto her port side where she has come to rest on her upper superstructure.

is beginning to disintegrate and offers little or no opportunity for penetration. This applies throughout most of the wreck, where a variety of doorways and hatches lie open. Entry into this wreck is, therefore, not recommended at all.

Right in front of the bridge at deck level, is an empty barbette onto which the missing machine gun was mounted. The remainder of the forward deck is largely clear except for some loose anchor chains which lead to some form of mechanical capstan. There is no visible windlass and the port anchor chain is run out and disappears across the seabed.

From the bows, we turn around and head for the stern. Swimming above the starboard side, the diver will immediately see the starboard anchor is tight up to the hawse pipe. Behind this is a large tear through the hull. This is the damage which caused the ship to sink when she was attacked in 1970 and the resultant hole is large enough for a diver to enter. Having been caused by an act of war, however, the edges of the hole are sharp and jagged with similar damage inside. Once again, therefore, entry is not recommended.

At 58m long, it is not a long swim back to the stern and this very different view of the wreck provides a great deal more to see and explore. All down the port side is a long companionway which was a feature of this type of ship. A large Paravane is still stored here and easily recognised by its torpedo shape. Once again, there are a few open doors offering a view into the ship's interior, although that is all they offer – just a view.

POSTSCRIPT – The opportunity to dive a former Soviet warship of any description is not a common one. Although the *Miniya* will never directly compete with any of the larger and more exciting shipwrecks found in Egyptian waters, she is nevertheless a superb little wreck and really worth a visit. A little too deep for that initial check-out dive at the start of a safari trip, this vessel provides an ideal way of rounding off such trips on return to Hurghada.

My diving partner pauses to study a feature of the *Miniya* approximately amidships during a swim towards the stern of the wreck.

Many of the hotels throughout Hurghada offer excellent facilities and first class beaches for the non-diver – or for those who prefer day-trips to the Dive Sites.

The Lighthouse on Big Brother Island.

From Hurghada –
south to Rocky Island

Rocky Island at dawn.

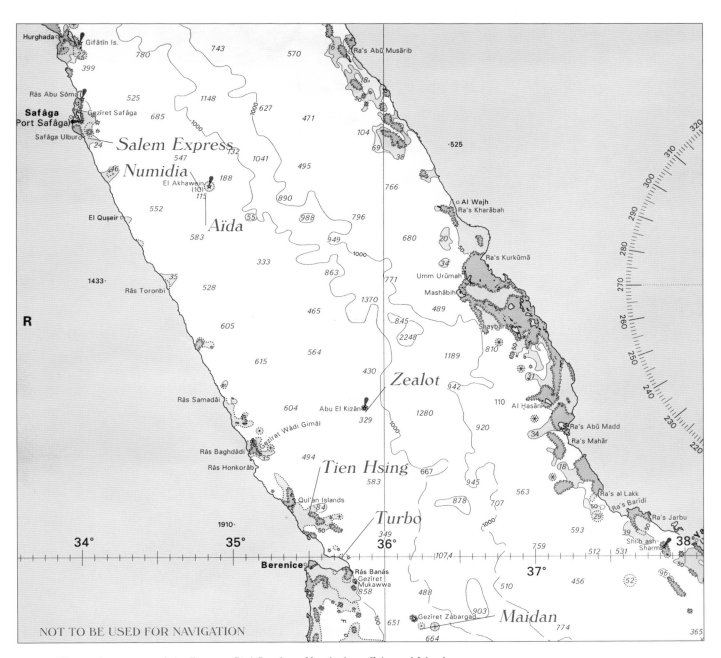

The southern sector of the Egyptian Red Sea from Hurghada to Zabargad Island. (Extract from Admiralty Chart 4704, United Kingdom Hydrographic Office)

Chapter XIV

SALEM EXPRESS

(GPS: 26° 38·367N, 34° 03·570E)

THE SHIP – Built by the French shipbuilding company, Forges & Ch de La Mediterranee, at La Seyne, the *Salem Express* was launched as the *Fred Scamaroni* in 1966. Described as a 'passenger roll-on, roll-off ferry,' she had capacity for 142 cars and 650 passengers and crew. She was later renamed *Nuits Saint George* in 1980, *Lord Sinai* in 1982 and *Al Tahra* in 1984 before finally becoming *Salem Express* in 1988. Although not a small ship by any standards, it is interesting to note her tonnage is smaller than that of the *Thistlegorm*. The *Salem Express* had three decks and her external dimensions were 100.29m x 17.8m with a draught of 4.92m and a displacement of 4,771 grt. Bow, stern and side doors were fitted with an up-lifting visor over the bows. She was powered by 4 x 8-cylinder diesel engines, reduction geared to drive two propellers. These produced a very handsome 14,880 hp and a top speed of 22 knots. The ship was also fitted with directional thrust propellers forward. The engines were built and fitted by Ch de L'Atlantique, also of La Seyne, France. The *Salem Express* was owned and operated by the Samatour

The passenger-vehicle ferry *Salem Express* as the *Fred Scamaroni* approaching the ferry terminal in Bastia, Corsica sometime prior to 1980.

(Ian Boyle/Simplon Postcards)

Shipping Company of Alexandria and based at Safaga at the time of her loss.

THE LOSS OF THE *SALEM EXPRESS* – The Saudi Arabian port of Jeddah is located on the eastern shores of the Red Sea at latitude 21° 28' North and it was here on 15 December 1991 that the *Salem Express* was loaded with vehicles and several hundred pilgrims. The passengers were in good heart and all dressed in their finest robes, as is always the case when returning from Mecca, a city that no non-believer is allowed to even view from a distance, let alone enter. Mecca is only a few miles from Jeddah where the Tomb of Eve, the mother of all mankind, is found. Together, these religious attractions make Jeddah the main port for all the many hundreds of thousands of pilgrims arriving by sea all year round.

Operating out of Safaga, the *Salem Express* was only one of many ferry services between Egypt and Saudi Arabia. Her captain was Hassan Moro, a very able and vastly experienced master mariner. Widely regarded throughout Egypt as a very fine seaman, Moro had even previously taught at the Egyptian Naval Academy. Though most of his working life was spent operating ships out of Alexandria, Moro had moved to Safaga to work for the Samatour Shipping Company and had been given command of the *Salem Express* in 1988. By 1991, therefore, he knew both his ship and the local waters, especially the route between Safaga and Jeddah, as well as any.

Perhaps too well! On the final stages of his return to Safaga, Captain Moro was in the habit of sailing between the Egyptian mainland and the treacherous Hyndman Reefs – which lie just offshore to the south of the port, a route which shaved a full two hours off the journey time. None of his fellow ships' captains would follow such a route; always remaining further offshore until they were able to take the designated path around the northern tip of Panorama Reef before steering a south-westerly course that would keep them in deeper water and further away from any of the many reefs nearby. It is interesting to note that, in the aftermath of the loss of the *Salem Express*, this route became compulsory for all big ships.

In December 1991, however, with the journey to Safaga being one of almost four hundred and fifty nautical miles, there was nobody to question the one man in charge of the *Salem Express* – the one man who understood the perils better than any other. By nightfall, the weather had deteriorated quite considerably with winds gusting to almost gale force. Many of those on board were deck-passengers and Moro was well aware of their discomfort on such a foul night. In conditions where many mariners would have found it difficult to distinguish between land, sea and reef, Moro crossed the Red Sea quickly and then deliberately hugged the Egyptian coast as he made his way northwards. In this way he was striving to provide his passengers with whatever protection he could from a Lee shore. As the vessel approached the Hyndman Reefs, it was close to midnight and no man alive could have distinguished reef from sea in those conditions. Sadly the ship was just a little off course and slightly east of Moro's normal route when the *Salem Express* struck the most southerly reef in the Hyndman group, with a heavy glancing blow.

The impact on the vessel was both immediate and twofold. Firstly, striking the reef caused the visor – which was so shaped as to become the ship's bows when in the closed position, to jolt open and raise. This allowed water into the car deck. A second, glancing blow ripped a hole in the hull on the forward starboard side. This was fatal and, on such a stormy night, catastrophic. As vast quantities of water swept into the ship from those two sources, it became every man for himself.

The vessel took on an immediate list to starboard, quickly exacerbated by water entering the car deck at an alarming pace. With the storm continuing unabated, there was instant panic among the passengers. In no time at all the vessel stalled as she continued to lean over towards the unforgiving sea. Within twenty minutes of striking the reef, the *Salem Express* sank, coming to rest in 30m of water on her starboard side. A small number of other vessels were moored in the immediate vicinity, safely tucked away on the lee side of the larger reefs in the area and grateful for the protection they afforded. One skipper who was keeping anchor watch later reported that he had watched the *Salem Express* as she approached. 'One moment she was there and the next she was gone,' he said.

Whilst many lives were lost when the ship sank, other passengers perished because they could not swim. For the remainder, however, the ordeal was not yet over. So swift had been the sinking that none of the lifeboats or life-rafts were properly launched. Those who would now survive, were on their own. The one crumb of comfort for those able to swim in the savage sea, was that the current was at least taking them towards the shore. Remarkably, one hundred and eighty people survived. Whilst a few were eventually plucked from the water, most had reached the coast and scrambled ashore unaided.

Officially, the vessel was carrying six hundred and fifty persons – 578 passengers and 72 crew, although many people insist she was carrying up to twice as many passengers. Whilst further speculation serves no useful purpose, there are those in Egypt who will categorically state that the actual death toll is in excess of one thousand. Whatever the truth, the official death toll was set at four hundred and seventy and it seems highly unlikely that the port officials of Jeddah would have allowed a grossly overloaded ship to depart.

With so many fatalities, many hundreds of relatives began demanding

This port side of the *Salem Express* reveals her substantial size.

The uppermost port propeller seen above the keel of the *Salem Express*.
The ship's single rudder is in the distance.

answers and, initially at least, the crew came in for considerable criticism when it became known that most of the lifeboats and life rafts had gone down with the ship. In all fairness, however, there was little time between the initial impact with the reef and the sinking to have achieved anything, especially as the ship came to have an immediate severe list to starboard. Of course, the one man responsible for everything which happened on that dreadful night was Captain Hassan Moro – and he went down with his ship. When the sun rose on the morning of 17 December, Safaga was already a veritable hive of activity with boats coming and going and military helicopters already in the air, all searching for survivors. It was not long, however, before the only task left was the gruesome one of recovering bodies.

One dive guide told me how he was diving in the vicinity and offered his services to the authorities. His party of scuba-diving holidaymakers had already agreed to assist. Soon they were joined by other boats and after recovering those bodies found in the immediate vicinity of the wreck, turned their attention to those which were still inside. From the cabins and accommodation all along the uppermost port side of the *Salem Express*, many bodies were recovered but as the divers worked their way gradually deeper and deeper down towards the inner reaches of the ship, it soon became clear that the task was becoming far too dangerous. A halt was called and the Egyptian Navy stepped in to seal the vessel from all further intrusion.

In answer to the most frequently asked question relating to the *Salem Express*, therefore: 'Yes – there are bodies still deep within the ship.' Furthermore, whilst divers are permitted to visit this shipwreck, entry into the wreck itself is strictly forbidden.

DIVING THE *SALEM EXPRESS* – This is a large ship which is found at a fairly uniform depth of 32m to the seabed. She lies squarely on her starboard side. In 2001, I noted that the visor was still found in the raised position, exactly as it would have been when in port to facilitate loading and unloading. A few months later I noted that a storm had forced it almost closed. Behind the visor, the large foredeck has few obstructions. There are two windlasses for the large anchors, both of which are fully retracted into their respective hawse-pipes. Immediately aft of these is the tall bridge-deck with its many rows of square windows, the upper-most row being the bridge. Several windows are now removed revealing how some divers have entered this and other parts of the wreck. Above is a small deck and mast.

Behind the bridge, is a sun deck with lifeboat davits on both sides. All the lifeboats on the uppermost (port) side are absent and the entire port side of the ship is a fairly uniform 10-12m for almost its entire length.

A shoal of Yellowfin Goatfish found near the stern of the *Salem Express*.

A considerable amount of debris has fallen to the seabed
from the after-deck of the *Salem Express*.

There is a long companionway with many doors that once gave access to
the ship's interior. Approximately amidships, the diver will find twin funnels. These are connected by a brace and on both sides of each funnel is
found the capital letter 'S' surrounded, most appropriately, by a wreath
of laurels. Immediately below the funnels are four lifeboats sitting on the
seabed. The after deck was where the main deck-passengers congregated.
Above this is a light framework over which sheets of blue corrugated
plastic were fixed to provide shelter from the heat of the day. Those corrugated sheets now litter the seabed below. It is also here that some personal belongings – such as a large stereo or the odd suitcase, are still
found.

As the diver approaches the square stern of the *Salem Express*, the sides begin to curve inwards making it quite easy to swim under the wreck. Emerging on the other side, the diver will immediately find the two huge propellers and an even bigger single rudder between them. Swimming forward towards the bows from this point, reveals a hull which is virtually featureless. Almost halfway there are stabilisers and, arriving at the bows themselves, there is that curious pointed part of the vessel onto which the visor once fitted snugly.

Below both the bows and the stern Blue-spotted stingray are regularly seen on the sand. The wreck itself is already covered in a hard coral and, being in a relatively sheltered location, is destined to eventually become a part of the Hyndman Reefs in its own right.

POSTSCRIPT – The very act of diving this particular shipwreck attracts controversy. There are those divers who refuse to visit this vessel – some of whom even object to those who do. Clearly such people feel the *Salem Express* should be placed out-of-bounds altogether. Each opinion is as valid as the next and this is not a question of right or wrong. As a professional underwater photo-journalist, my job is to report the facts and not glorify this particular shipwreck in any way. I do believe all divers should accept the fact that the *Salem Express* does exist and that divers are permitted to visit the wreck provided they do not enter within. In this way we can all respect the decisions of individual divers who decide whether or not they wish to see this wreck. What I do find curious, however, is how some of those who insist we should not dive the *Salem Express* are very happy to move on and visit wrecks such as the *Carnatic* where only thirty-one people died or the *Thistlegorm* where the number was just nine! Of course, these are not such recent tragedies and, unlike the *Salem Express*, there are no personal possessions – such as a radio or perhaps a shoe, found on the seabed nearby...

This access hatch was originally sealed by Egyptian military divers to prevent unauthorised access into the *Salem Express*. It has since been moved to one side.

• Chapter XV •

NUMIDIA

(GPS: 26° 18·850N, 54° 50·005E)

THE SHIP – Officially described as a 'steel screw steamship,' the *Numidia* was completed in February 1901. She was a general cargo vessel with both ship and engines built by D & W Henderson & Co. of Glasgow. A very large ship for her day, her dimensions were 137.4m x 16.7m with a draught of 9.2m and a displacement of 6,399 grt. She had 4 cargo holds – two forward and two aft of a central bridge deck which also included extensive accommodation for a small number of passengers plus a very large crew. The ship was fitted with a 3-cylinder triple-expansion steam engine capable of producing 447 hp and a top speed of 10 knots. The *Numidia* was owned and operated by the Anchor Line of Glasgow throughout her short life.

THE LOSS OF THE *NUMIDIA* – On 28 February 1901 the *Numidia* set out from Glasgow on her maiden voyage. She was a well-found ship and the lengthy journey from Glasgow and Liverpool, through the Suez Canal to Bombay and Calcutta before returning to the Clyde, was an excellent opportunity for both captain and crew to get to know the brand new vessel. Her second voyage, however, would be very different! Having already

The *Assyria* – only sister ship of the *Numidia*. (Scottish Maritime Museum)

arrived at Liverpool for additional cargo, on 6 July 1901 Captain John Craig ordered the mooring lines slipped. He was standing beside the pilot as the vessel moved slowly into the River Mersey and then out into the Irish Sea.

The *Numidia* was carrying a general cargo of 7,000 tons and a crew of ninety-seven. There were no passengers. Over the next several days, each different leg of the journey – down to the Straits of Gibraltar, the entire length of the Mediterranean Sea and then through the Suez Canal, were all uneventful and the ship finally cleared Suez at 02.48 hrs 19 July 1901. She then made good time down the Gulf of Suez and by 19.00 hrs that evening, Shadwan Island was already two miles abeam. It was at this point the master set a course of S. 31°E (true) to be steered for a distance of 47 nautical miles, as measured by the patent log trailed astern. The weather was recorded as fine with a fresh breeze from NNW.

At 2300 hrs the course was altered to S. 30°E (true) and at 01.00 hrs 20 July, the light on Big Brother Island was sighted off the port bow. Captain Craig was on the bridge at this time and, observing the light's bearing, instructed the helmsman to alter course to S. 27°E (true). Second Mate James Tulloch was officer of the watch and the Captain made a point of turning to him and specifically informing him of this change of course – even though Tulloch had clearly observed the corrections being made. Craig then told Tulloch that this course would take the ship over one mile to the west of Big Brother Island. The master then retired to his cabin, leaving instructions that he was to be called when the Brother's Light was abeam.

At 02.10 hrs Craig was awoken by the shock of the *Numidia* crashing onto rocks. Hurrying to the bridge, he found his ship hard aground on Big Brother Island – less than 150 metres from the lighthouse. Taking charge of the situation, Craig noted their heading was due south, the helm was set at hard-a-port and the engines were already going full astern. The engines then remained like this for another two hours until it was realised the ship was stuck fast and they were stopped. By this time the ship was taking on water all the way back from the aft part of No. 1 Hold. As a precaution, therefore, all boats were swung out and provisional preparations made for abandoning ship.

At 07.30 hrs the SS *Rhipens* came in sight and was used to send despatches to Suez for urgent assistance. After she moved off, a large number of the crew were landed and a system of communications established between ship and shore. Other vessels then arrived and every effort was made to refloat the *Numidia* without success. Eventually accepting his ship was lost, the master allowed these vessels to rescue his crew, although he remained on the island for a further seven weeks during which time he supervised the salvage of the greater portion of the

Some time after the *Numidia* ran aground, her back broke in two at a point immediately in front of the bridge with everything aft of that break sinking against the Reef. Note how the handrail is broken on the far side.

The entire wreck of the *Numidia* is covered in a rich assortment of hard and soft corals. The wreck also enjoys some of the clearest underwater visibility found anywhere in the Red Sea.

cargo. At some later date, the *Numidia* broke in two at a point immediately in front of the bridge with everything aft of that break sinking against the Reef.

THE BOARD OF TRADE ENQUIRY – The formal Board of Trade Enquiry was held in Glasgow on 23 and 24 October 1901. Those appointed to sit in judgement commented on the conflict of evidence between the Master and Second Mate as to precisely what instructions were given before Captain Craig left the Bridge in the early hours of 20 July. They later voiced the opinion that the Second Mate had probably fallen asleep at his post and had failed to make good the courses set by Captain Craig. Nevertheless, it emerged that the Second Mate must have been awake at 01.30 hrs (a full forty minutes before the ship struck) because at this time he suddenly altered the course to S. 22°E on his own initiative. Why he did not immediately inform the master of this change was never explained.

The question before the court, therefore, was simple. Was the loss of the *Numidia* caused by a wrongful act or error on the part of either the Master or Second Mate, or by a combination of both? The court's findings were clear enough. Firstly, they were not satisfied that the Master had taken sufficient care when altering the course to pass Big Brother Island, in that the alteration should have been to a greater extent in order to ensure the vessel passed well clear. They also stated he should have remained on the bridge until Big Brother Light was passed. These, however, were only comments and did not attract any punishment. With regard to the Second Mate, they concluded he had failed to keep sufficient distance from the Brothers Islands and neglected to call the master when the course was last altered by himself. They duly suspended his certificate for a period of nine months.

In reviewing all the available evidence from that enquiry, it should be remembered that in these pre-satellite and pre-GPS days of seafaring, it was common practise for all ships' masters to haul up close to any remote island in order to provide themselves with the most accurate fix of their position at that specific time. For Craig to have set a course which would bring his ship to within a mile of any prominent island would, therefore, ordinarily have been an act of good seamanship. It should also be noted that on this particular ship, the helm was located at the back of the bridge from where the helmsman was unable to see out. It later emerged that when he first came on duty, James Tulloch gave the helmsman a severe reprimand over a very minor matter. Thus a situation existed

Looking directly at the north-west coast of Big Brother Island. It was on the reef to the left of the island that the *Numidia* ran aground and later sank in 1901.

whereby Tulloch was clearly upset over something the helmsman may or may not have done and the helmsman was also aggrieved at the treatment he had received. This created an unfortunate atmosphere whereby the only two men on duty for the next four hours were not even speaking to each other – something which might have kept the Second Mate from falling asleep.

When the Captain left the bridge, it would seem that Mr. Tulloch sat down in the captain's chair and eventually dozed off. Then, on suddenly waking at 01.30 hrs, found himself in a position whereby he had failed to follow orders. In a desperate bid to rectify matters – without the master discovering his incompetence, he then tried to bring the ship's heading gradually round to where it should have been, but his actions only made matters worse and the ship was lost.

DIVING THE *NUMIDIA* – I have always been intrigued by this particular shipwreck – simply because so many so-called facts did not add up. Consider this: The *Numidia* was over 137m long. Various published accounts of the ship, however, have stated: The broken bows are found in 8m, the wreck lies up the reef at an almost vertical angle and the ship's stern is found at 80m. On top of that, another source also informed me the *Numidia* is found in two halves, with the front half lying up the reef and the rear half some distance away. Later this was changed to the other way around – but the relevance was that the two halves of this ship were being described as two quite separate dives.

I always like to complete as much research as possible into any shipwreck prior to seeing the vessel itself. With so much conflicting information, by the time I found myself approaching this wreck for the very first time, I really was looking forward to taking a very close look. In so doing, I made an important discovery.

We were taken to the *Numidia* in small groups by RHIB. Just as soon as I saw the wreck, I followed the port side all the way down to 65m from where I could see the seabed level out at the base of the reef. This was still some 10-15m below, but I could clearly see the rounded stern of the ship and her rudder and propeller sitting on the sand. I had been underwater for less than four minutes and already one of the many questions in my mind had been answered; this was definitely the rear of the *Numidia*. Incredibly, even at this depth, we found examples of coral growth which simply became more and more prolific as we ascended. This wreck sits on a prime example of coral reef which, together with the wreck, attract only the most excellent examples of fishes. The coral grouper were particularly outstanding – and as big and colourful as any found elsewhere in the Red Sea. Various species of shark and other pelagics are also frequently seen.

One of the tall ventilation towers which provided
fresh air below decks throughout the ship.

A view from port to starboard across the rear
of the bridge deck of the *Numidia*.

Getting to work with my camera, I was immediately struck by the similarities between this wreck and the *Aïda*. Once again we had a steel-hulled vessel on which the wooden decking had disappeared. What remained was a three-dimensional steel framework, through which the diver could easily gain access to all parts of the ship. The largest space on the after-deck was clearly the entrance to No. 4 Hold. Immediately in front of this is the mainmast – still intact as far as the crosstrees and still standing proud. With the decks almost vertical, this mast has remained at this angle for over one hundred years and is yet another example of a well-made item still defying the laws of gravity. Immediately below the mast are some very large deck winches which once supplied the lifting power for the cargo booms. Those booms, however, were nowhere to be seen.

After passing over the open No. 3 Hold, we approached the rear of the raised central bridge deck. Lifeboat davits on both sides were all swung out and large air vents – some broken, some still intact, occupied the deck space. By now the wreck was an incredible confusion of colour with the soft corals adding hues of every shade from deep purple to light green as their true colours benefited from exposure to artificial light. No sooner had I photographed the remains of the funnel, I saw we had reached the end of that which is recognisable as a ship. We were now at 12m and over to the starboard side I saw the first of two pairs of railway engine wheels with offset axles. These were being carried as deck cargo and destined for India. The second pair are now firmly embedded into the reef at a depth of only 8m – some distance away.

So, the first of a number of dives on the *Numidia* was over and we now had plenty of time to think about what we had just seen and experienced. As I have said, this was clearly the rear half of the ship. The shallowest elements of the wreck had clearly suffered from being in such shallow water and it took several dives before I could be certain of what precisely I was looking at – and all the time I kept wondering about the rest of the ship. Just where was it?

During the following dives we had plenty of time to study the reef over to our left as we swam back to our dive boat time and again. Here and there we could see the occasional piece of a ship. Then, suddenly, I took a very close look. Surely that was an encrusted porthole. Then I saw another and a third and all at uniform distances apart. On the next dive, I ignored the 'wreck' and inspected the reef on which it foundered – and there it was, the rest of the ship. All of it.

Only now could I see exactly what had happened to this vessel. The *Numidia* drove hard onto the shallow reef at the northern end of Big Brother island. Here she became firmly fixed and, as she began to settle by the stern, so the front 'half' of the ship sat down on that reef. The remainder of the ship – from a point just in front of the bridge deck all the way back to the stern, was then suspended over the deep precipice above the edge of an almost vertical reef.

Eventually, the ship's back was broken and that rear half fell down the reef – exactly as she is found to this day. But!, the remainder of the wreck never moved. Instead, it fell victim to successive winter storms until the last remnants finally disappeared beneath the surface to be claimed by a combination of water and coral. Almost as though she had been pounded flat by powerful steam-hammers for over one hundred years, the rest of this fabulous ship is still there – compressed onto the reef itself until it became almost indistinguishable. In short, the missing part was never missing at all, it is still there waiting to be investigated. All things considered, this is one of the most incredible shipwrecks it has ever been my privilege to visit.

The *Numidia* is easily one of the most beautiful shipwrecks in the world. The railings, mast, lifeboat davits, windlasses, deck winches and even the decks themselves have all become part of a living reef of such vibrancy it is easy to lose sight of the fact she is also a most spectacular wreck dive. If ever there was a competition to find the most beautiful shipwreck in the entire world, the *Numidia* would certainly be on any short-list of finalists because I have yet to see anything better.

POSTSCRIPT – Captain John Craig was born in Glasgow in 1845 and obtained his Master's Certificate (No. 85545) there in 1872 at the age of twenty-seven years. Prior to the *Numidia*, he commanded the *Algeria* for three years from 1896 and joined the *Numidia* for her maiden voyage in February 1901. After the loss of the *Numidia* and his strenuous efforts to salvage as much cargo as possible, there is no record of John Craig ever having returned to sea.

One of at least two pairs of railway engine wheels which were being carried as deck cargo on the *Numidia*. Note the flange on the nearest wheel.

© RICO 2004

Chapter XVI

AïDA

(GPS: 26° 18·762N, 34° 50·051E)

THE SHIP – Technically described as a passenger freighter, the *Aïda* was ordered by the Egyptian Ports and Lighthouses Administration from Ateliers et Chantiers de la Loire of Nantes, France – who built both ship and engines. Launched in 1911, her dimensions were 75.1m x 9.7m with a draught of 7m (unladen) and a displacement of 1,428 grt. She was powered by a 3-cylinder triple-expansion steam engine capable of producing 229 hp and a top speed of 9 knots. For some years prior to the launch of the *Aïda*, the production of steamships throughout Europe had moved right away from the classic sailing ship lines which dominated earlier craft. Whilst the *Rosalie Moller* (completed in 1910), for example, had two masts, she was never rigged for sail. Although never intended, it is curious to note how the style of the hull of the *Aïda* looks as though she could have been converted to sail at any time.

HISTORICAL BACKGROUND – From the moment she was launched, the *Aïda* appeared in every issue of Lloyd's Register of Shipping until

The *Aïda* in 1911, during the fitting-out phase of her construction in Nantes, France. Although never rigged for sail, the ship possessed beautiful sailing lines (*Historie de la construction navale à Nantes*)

1929/30, when she was removed. The next time she came to prominence in the UK was in a 'Most Secret' document, dated 8 October 1941 which formed part of the official Royal Navy War Diary. In this instance, a number of ships damaged and sunk in the Gulf of Suez were reported as follows:

War Diary
                                                    Most Secret
                                                    8. 10. 1941
                                                    Wednesday

SITUATION REPORT

Egypt and   *S. S. ROSALIE MOLLER* was sunk by enemy air attack
Canal Area.   on Anchorage H. between 0045B and 0140B. *S. S. AIDA*
                (Ports and Lights vessel) was sunk at Zafarana
                Anchorage by H. E. III which crashed at the same time
                after hitting *AIDA*'s mast. *S. S. AIDA* can be salved.

In the early hours of 6 October 1941 German bombers from Crete sunk the *Thistlegorm* and now, almost exactly forty-eight hours later, had returned to seek out fresh targets. As one aircraft attacked and sank the *Rosalie Moller*, another Heinkel He III attacked the *Aïda*. The method of attack was always the same. The pilot would approach each ship from ahead or astern as he continued to lose altitude. Then, just as he was approaching the target ship, he would release his bombs right above her. In the case of the *Thistlegorm* and *Rosalie Moller*, they were both at anchor and provided the German pilots with sitting targets. When it came to the *Aïda*, however, she was underway, thus allowing her master to take evasive action. Just as the bombs were released so the Captain of the *Aïda* ordered an emergency 'Hard-a-Starboard' and that manoeuvre resulted in both bombs missing his ship, though they did explode close enough to cause some damage. The speed at which the ship turned also caught the German pilot by surprise and he was unable to avoid hitting the ship's mast before crashing into the sea.

Thinking very quickly, the master of the *Aïda* continued on his new course and headed straight for shallow water where he beached his ship. There were no casualties from the *Aïda*, though only four of the aircraft's five-crew members were eventually taken prisoner, after making their own way ashore.

This was all at a time when Allied shipping was being lost at an unsustainable rate throughout the world, and every effort was made to salvage any vessel or part of a vessel that was not considered a total loss. Consequently, the *Aïda* was refloated, repaired and lived to sink another day. Having already been officially described as sunk during WW2, how-

Big Brother Island – viewed from the south. Beyond the jetty shown on the left of the island,
the *Aïda* was wrecked in 1957 and beyond that the *Numidia* was lost in 1901.

ever, gave rise to speculative accounts that the shipwreck now found off Big Brother Island must be the *Aïda II*. This is incorrect although other vessels called *Aïda* have remained in use in Egypt and it is understood the *Aïda IV* is a tugboat currently in service in Alexandria.

THE BROTHERS ISLANDS – Approximately sixty miles southeast of Safaga are two islands where the surrounding waters are almost 1000m deep. These are the Brothers Islands and are as remote as islands get. The larger of the two is called Big Brother and is immediately recognisable by the presence of a large lighthouse. This island is located just over a mile to the north west of Little Bother, which, as the name suggests, is much smaller. On the sheltered west-facing coast of Big Brother is a very old jetty. This provides access to the island and is in regular use by a combination of those responsible for maintaining the lighthouse and a contingent of Egyptian soldiers stationed there for two or three months at a time.

THE LOSS OF THE *AïDA* – At some time after WW2, the *Aïda* was transferred to Egyptian Marine and regularly used for ferrying troops to some of Egypt's remote outstations. This is how the ship came to be off Big Brother Island on 15 September 1957. She was carrying a total of 157 persons, including her crew, at the time. According to *The Illustrated London News*, there were heavy storms on that day and it would seem that, despite an unfavourable sea state, the Captain was determined to reach the jetty in order to complete the tasks he had been set. In so doing, however, he struck the reef on which the jetty stands. The damage to the ship's hull was considerable and the *Aïda* was immediately down by the stern as she began to take on water. Her master had no option but to send out a distress call. The Norwegian tugboat, *Bergehus* responded immediately and managed to rescue seventy-seven of those on board. The remainder, including the Captain, all scrambled safely ashore, from where everyone was later rescued.

Moving almost imperceptibly, the *Aïda* began to drift slowly north as she became increasingly further down by the stern. She then became lodged on a shallow reef from where every effort was made to prevent the ship from becoming a total loss. The inexorable combination of her damaged hull resting on an unforgiving reef coupled with continual heavy seas, however, soon proved the strength of nature over man and she was finally abandoned as a constructive total loss. It was now only a matter of time before the ship would sink and she remained where she was for no more than two or three days before finally disappearing from sight.

Underwater, the ship was at a very precarious angle. Still trapped by a ledge at about 12m, the *Aïda* was hanging vertically down a steep reef.

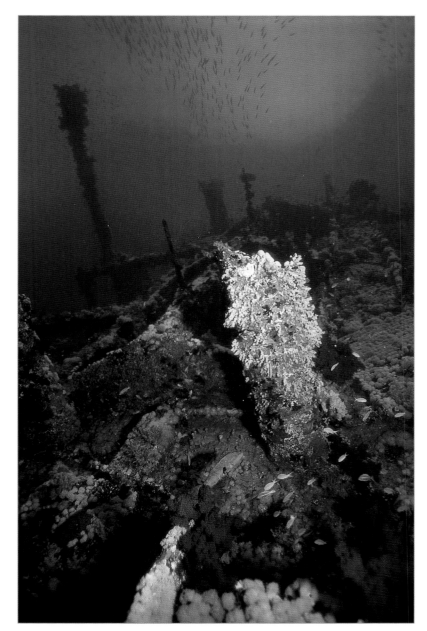

Looking up the wreck of the *Aïda* across the top of the ship's central bridge deck with those large open hatches located immediately above the engine room.

The view up the starboard side of the *Aïda* with lifeboat davits in the distance.

Still at the mercy of heavy seas, therefore, the ship eventually broke completely in two – with the aft section falling down the reef until the stern came to rest at 56m. Over ensuing years, the remainder of the ship continued to be battered until only the engines remained, still firmly lodged on that ledge at 12m.

DIVING THE *AÏDA* – On my first visit to the *Aïda*, I was diving from that outstanding safari boat *My Rosetta* which was skilfully moored off the southern tip of Big Brother island by her skipper Captain Gafar Abrahim – always known as 'The Gaffer'. From here we were bussed to the wreck in small groups using the boat's RHIB. Ignoring the engine block at 12m, our main interest was the wreck itself and I immediately headed straight down to the deepest part – from where I could work my way slowly back to the surface. Here I found the beautifully rounded stern with handrails and bollards still intact. The depth was 56m and both rudder and propeller were still in place, though half-buried in the sand.

My first impression was a lasting one. This was a steel-hulled vessel with wooden planking. After so many years underwater, however, those wooden decks have gone revealing a steel framework which provides easy access to all parts of the ship. Such is the appearance of the steel supports as they criss-cross the ship, she looks almost as though she was constructed from a giant Meccano set – except that this Meccano set now enjoys a whole new lease of life as an extension to the adjacent reef. Even at 56m, the coral growth is truly outstanding and grows more vibrant with each passing metre as we slowly ascend. Looking around I was also pleased to see that this was where the really big boys hang out and very few Grouper from anywhere in the Red Sea compete with these fellows in terms of size.

Being so far offshore, the Brothers do not suffer from any of the pollutants that plague inshore diving the world over. Here, rich nutrients sweep down from the north to provide the diver with one of the most abundant areas of coral growth found anywhere. Throughout the many years the *Aïda* has been underwater, she has slowly been transformed into a thing of great beauty – a solid base for the most magnificent examples of hard and soft corals. That, coupled with a wide variety of exciting fishes,combine to make the *Aïda* one of the best wreck and reef dives around.

Halfway up the afterdeck, are the remains of the rear mast. Like a number of other masts described in this book, this also sticks out from the wreck at an angle of something like 55-60 degrees from upright and also continues to defy the inevitable laws of gravity and deterioration as it does so. Immediately below the mast are all the usual deck winches which once supplied the lifting power. At 35m we approached the rear of

A closer view of any of the deck detail of the *Aïda* reveals a
colourful assortment of hard and soft corals.

tion also creates a dive site of equal interest to those who enjoy wreck
diving as well as those who prefer reefs, corals and fishes. Furthermore,
her remote location also means she is largely overlooked – if only because
the majority of wreck divers who visit Egypt prefer the more numerous
shipwrecks found north of Hurghada. This absence of divers in large
numbers enables both the *Aïda* and *Numidia* to enjoy very high reputa-
tions as two of Egypt's unspoilt shipwrecks.

POSTSCRIPT – The name of the ship's master at the time she was lost
was not made public and no official comment about the sinking was ever
made except to record the cause as a 'Navigational Error'.

the bridge deck. Lifeboat davits on both sides are swung out and large air
vents – both intact and broken are found on the upper deck. The powerful modelling lights from my twin Ikelite sub-strobes bring everything
attached to this wreck into life – a living confusion of colour with the soft
corals in particular adding various shades of almost every colour imagi-
nable as they reveal themselves.

At 28m, we reach the end of the wreckage. This is where the ship
broke in two. The bridge would have been a wooden structure on top of
the leading edge of this section but, alas, is no more. Immediately below
the accommodation is a large open space, the identity of which was very
easy to determine. The many items scattered around this shell-like opening include pipes, valves, ladders and walkways – all betraying the simple
fact this was once the engine room. How Mother Nature could have
wrenched the engines from this ship and leave them on a ledge at a depth
of 12m above is hard to imagine. Nevertheless, even without her engines,
there is still plenty to interest those with inquisitive minds and a good
torch.

From the moment I first saw the *Aïda*, I was aware she was something
special as she occupied her very own space at the lower end of an almost
vertical reef between 28 and 56m. Like the *Numidia*, it is a combination
of her being a man-made object, a prolific coral growth and her offshore
location which makes her a truly outstanding shipwreck. This combina-

• Chapter XVII •

TURBO

(GPS: 24° 00·408N, 35° 37·979E)

A TALE OF TWO SHIPWRECKS – In recent years, there has been considerable confusion as to the true identity of this wreck. So much so, had she not been eventually correctly identified, I am sure she would have been given the local name of 'Mr Confusion'. The wreckage comprises the rear half of a tanker of moderate size. From my own first initial survey, which was long before the vessel was correctly identified, the information available was that this was a tanker of a design where the bridge was located amidships and her engine room plus additional accommodation was at the rear. The problems with formal identification, however, were twofold. Firstly, the ship had, for whatever reason, been cut in two immediately aft of the bridge with everything forward of that cut missing altogether. What we had, therefore, was the rear half of a ship minus her bridge deck. The second problem arose from spurious accounts of this wreck being wrongly identified as the *Atlas* – a ship, which had been torpedoed and sunk in 1940, over six hundred and eighty miles further south, off the coast of Yemen.

The *Turbo* photographed in 1912. Note how very similar this ship is to the *Scalaria* (see Appendix). (National Museums Liverpool)

THE RED SEA – During my research I was quickly able to discount the *Atlas* but, in order to explain why, we need to understand a little something about the Red Sea. This is an inland sea which separates Africa from Arabia. It is important to note that no rivers run into the Red Sea. At the northern end, the Gulf of Aqaba is that narrow strip of very deep water, to the east of the Sinai Peninsula. The Gulf of Suez is somewhat similar, though larger and not as deep, to the west of that same peninsula and provides the vital link to the Suez Canal. At its southern extreme, the Red Sea ends at a narrow point between South Yemen and Djibouti. This is where the Gulf of Aden begins and beyond that lies the Indian Ocean.

Measured from the southern tip of the Sinai Peninsula to the Gulf of Aden, the Red Sea is over 1,100 nautical miles long and more than 220 miles across at its widest point (latitude 16°N). Throughout its entire length, the Red Sea is bordered by fringing reefs, numerous coral outcrops, individual reefs and remote islands. These are far more numerous in the southern Red Sea where the charts record varying depths of very shallow water (as shallow as 3m!), stretching all the way out as far as 90 miles from the Ethiopian mainland on the western side and 75 miles from the southern most point of Saudi Arabia on the opposite shores.

These shallow reefs, therefore, combine to reduce the navigable channels of the Red Sea by one hundred and sixty-five miles in those latitudes. With no rivers to affect the flow of water, currents and tides are created by water being lost through evaporation. As a general rule, this creates a situation whereby prevailing currents flow down the centre of the Red Sea from north to south and up the east and west coasts from south to north. Any ship abandoned in a floating condition is not going to travel over six hundred and eighty miles north where, amongst other things, it would have provided a serious and constant danger to shipping. On the contrary, any such abandoned ship would either drift further south or become wrecked on any one of the numerous and very treacherous reefs to the east and west.

THE *ATLAS* – Officially described as a steel screw steamer, the *Atlas* was a bulk petroleum tanker built by R. Craggs and Sons of Tees Dockyard, Middlesbrough and launched in July 1909 as the *Conrad Mohr*. She was renamed *Irini* in 1930 and finally became the *Atlas* in 1935. Her dimensions were 105.18m x 14.63m with a draught of 8.68m and a displacement of 4,009 grt. Lloyd's Register of Shipping 1937-38 reveals her machinery to have been located aft and consisted of a 3-cylinder triple-expansion steam engine which produced 326 hp and top speed of 7.5 knots. She was owned and operated by the Soc. Anon. Hellénique Maritime 'Transpetrol' of Piraeus, Greece at the time of her loss.

When her skeleton crew abandoned ship, they were taken off by the *Gladys Moller* which had been towing the *Turbo* until she foundered. Because the lifeboats were not used, the davits are not swung out.

According to a report entitled Axis Submarine Successes, the *Atlas* was torpedoed by the Italian submarine *Guglielmotti* on 6 September 1940 and logged by the submarine's commander as 'sinking at position 15° 50'N, 41° 50'E in deep water off the coast of Yemen.' Other sources state that, on 6 September 1940 the *Atlas* was straggling behind north-bound convoy BN4 in the southern Red Sea when she was torpedoed and sunk. Convoy escorts returned to the scene and rescued survivors.

Both the position given by the Italian submarine commander and the fact that the *Atlas* was recorded as sinking are confirmed by Naval Staff, Trade Division and the UK Hydrographic Office. The latter having also stated: 'None of the references has any mention of the vessel breaking in two or being towed.' Furthermore, none of the Royal Navy escort ships reported any wreckage still afloat.

Plotted onto Admiralty Chart 4704, the position given by the submarine commander places the *Atlas* due east of Centre Peak Island, off the coast of South Yemen. I then obtained an accurate GPS position of the half tanker wreck at Râs Banas, before that too was plotted onto the same Chart. The distance between the two marks is 680 nautical miles. In summary, there is no record of any part of the *Atlas* either having been salvaged or remaining afloat after she was attacked and sunk and that vessel will now be found – exactly where she fell, off the coast of Yemen some 680 nautical miles south of Râs Banas.

Whilst it was clear to me, therefore, that this half tanker could not possibly be the *Atlas*, I had to recognise certain similarities between that ship and the unidentified wreck. As the search for information continued, I was ever hopeful of finding an answer. In early 2002, I took another look at Roger Jordan's most excellent book *The World's Merchant Fleets 1939*. This book has proved to be one of the most useful tools in terms of researching ships lost during WW2 and lists over 6,000 ships belonging to the merchant fleets of the world and their wartime fates. I began by reading the 41 pages which give the briefest possible details of those British and Commonwealth ships lost – and how they were lost. I had missed it before, but this time I noticed a curious entry on page 514 which reads: '*Turbo* 20.8.41 Torpedoed by aircraft, badly damaged, 32 08N 31 57E; ar Port Said 4.4.42 when in tow heavy weather, broke in two 25 16N 35 25E, forepart shelled, sunk afterpart foundered.'

The first time I read this item, I had noticed how the first of those two quoted positions was in the Mediterranean. Being so far from the Red Sea I then dismissed the *Turbo* as a possible contender. On this occasion, however, I realised how the second position given was well down in the Red Sea. On checking my charts I found it was something like 74 nautical miles due north of our wrecked tanker. It was time to take a closer interest in this *Turbo*.

THE *TURBO* – Lloyd's Register of Shipping 1912/13 (Vol. 1) reveals the *Turbo* was built in Sunderland by Sir James Laing & Sons Ltd and launched in August 1912. She was a bulk petroleum tanker fitted for liquid fuels. Her bridge was located amidships and her machinery aft. Her dimensions are recorded as 374ft 2in (114.08m) x 50ft 8in (15.45m) with a draught of 27ft 4in (8.33m) and a displacement of 4,900 grt. Her engines were built by J. Dickinson & Sons (also of Sunderland) and comprised a 3-cylinder triple-expansion steam engine, providing a top speed of 10 knots. The ship was registered in London and went into immediate service with the Anglo Saxon Petroleum Company which later became part of Shell.

The *Turbo* then appears in every issue of Lloyd's Register of Shipping for 30 years until the 1940/41 (Vol. 2) edition where we find she is still sailing under the same name, is still powered by the same engines and still retains the same owners. Interestingly, therefore, both the *Atlas* and the *Turbo* were bulk petroleum tankers, were both built in the North East of England within 3 years of each other, both conformed to the same general design and were both of similar size and appearance. That, however, is where all similarities end – especially when I unearthed the story of how the *Turbo* was lost.

THE LOSS OF THE *TURBO* – Lloyd's Service Lists for 1939/45 shows the *Turbo* having been requisitioned under the TRS (Tanker Requisition Scheme) and later designated as TW – an official abbreviation used to denote Total Loss Due to War Causes. The ship was, therefore, being used by the Ministry of Transport at the time of her loss. Unfortunately, details about the actual loss itself are sparse because people were averse to committing anything to paper at the time. On the one hand, they did not want the enemy to know which ships were lost and which were not and on the other hand, they did not want to publicise anything which would have an adverse affect on public morale.

What I did piece together from various documents held at the National Maritime Museum and the Public Records Office, however, is as follows; In August 1941 the *Turbo* was in the Mediterranean on passage from Haifa for Alexandria with 7,500 tons of Admiralty fuel. Like the *Thistlegorm*, she had been fitted with a raised gun platform over the after deck and on which were mounted unspecified weapons. In addition to her crew of forty-two, she was also carrying ten Royal Navy DEMS personnel. DEMS was the acronym for Defensively Equipped Merchant Ships and the term was applied to those RN personnel assigned to man the guns on such ships.

On 20 August 1941, the ship was attacked by enemy aircraft, torpedoed and badly damaged. It seems her entire crew abandoned ship and were all safely rescued. The ship itself, however, did not sink and is next recorded as having arrived at Port Said on 21 August. Whether she was brought into port by her original crew or another crew from, perhaps, a salvage vessel, is not known. Nevertheless, the ship arrived in very poor condition. Her cargo was then offloaded and it was decided she would be towed to Aden for either repairs or scrapping. The *Turbo* subsequently left Port Said on 23 September 1941 and arrived at Suez the following day where she remained for the next six months. Being in short supply, her deck guns were removed either at Port Said or Suez.

The ship finally departed Suez on 1 April 1941 for Aden in tow of *Gladys Moller* (coincidentally owned and operated by the same company as the *Rosalie Moller*). Towing any ship is a slow and laborious task and by 4 April, they were still in the Egyptian Red Sea when they encountered stormy weather. As conditions worsened, so the state of the *Turbo* gave cause for great concern. There was nothing the master of the *Gladys Moller* could do except recover the skeleton crew from the *Turbo* and watch as the ship broke in two. The stricken ship was then cast adrift at position 25° 16N 35° 25E, leaving the *Gladys Moller* to ride out the storm unhindered. The responsibility of the master of the *Gladys Moller*, however, did not end there and at some point he informed the authorities about the danger to shipping posed by the two halves of this rather large ship. The remainder of the story is then found as follows:

After the ship was lost, the following addendum was issued to Lloyd's Casualty Lists of 20 August 1941 (being the date of the original attack in the Mediterranean):

'*Turbo* on tow 4th April 1942 & cast adrift because of heavy weather. Forepart sunk as it was a danger to navigation. Afterpart is presumed to have foundered.'

From piecing together each snippet of information, it would appear that an RN vessel arrived on the scene and sunk the forepart of the ship with gunfire before conducting a search for the remainder of the wreck. Having failed to find that wreckage, the afterpart of the *Turbo* was 'presumed to have foundered.' Bearing in mind how prevailing currents flow from north to south in the Red Sea, it is easy to understand now how the rear half of the *Turbo* was carried south until it really did founder – on the north-facing side of that small spit of land known as Râs Banas.

Add to all this, the fact that our mystery wreck still has a gun platform in place over the afterdeck – there never was a gun platform on the *Atlas*!, and I was more than satisfied that the half tanker wreck at Râs Banas was indeed the remains of the *Turbo* and that the *Atlas* remains over 680 miles away.

DIVING THE *TURBO* – It was August 2002 when I first saw this wreck. I was visiting the southern Egyptian Red Sea as the guest on board the ever-beautiful safari boat *My Rosetta*. Our Dive Guide was the charming Monika Hofbauer who told me how she was first shown the wreck in early 1997 after a very good friend – who had been diving the wreck for some years, revealed its location.

Eventually we arrived over the site of what was then called the 'Mystery Tanker' which lies against an inshore reef on the northern side of Râs Banas. Even from the surface, we could see a substantial shipwreck resting on the seabed below. Just as soon as we got wet, it was clear to everyone we were looking at the rear half of a tanker of moderate size. I say moderate because she had clearly been a fairly big ship – though small by tanker standards. The wreck was approximately 70m long and lies parallel to the nearby fringing reef, leaning away from that reef well over onto its port side. Later that day, I wrote in my log 'She was a type of tanker with the bridge deck located amidships and was broken immediately aft of that bridge. The break is neat and clean, almost as though a giant knife had sliced through the vessel. Everything forward of that break is completely missing.'

Starting at the forward end, an inspection of the damage shows the starboard side to have been neatly cut in a straight line all the way down the hull from top to bottom. The ship had 5 cargo holds – two fore and two aft of the central bridge deck with No. 3 Hold located below the bridge. Having, therefore, separated immediately aft of the bridge, the cut runs right through No. 3 Hold. Curiously, the severed ends are neatly folded back into the ship and onto themselves – almost as though they had been deliberately crimped.

Only the last 2 metres or so of No. 3 Hold remain and, looking into the gaping hole, we can see the forward bulkhead of No. 4 Hold with an inspection ladder running all the way up from floor to deck hatch. On both sides, tucked immediately below the main decks, are the remains of smaller, separate cargo spaces – something like the tanker equivalent of 'tween decks. These were used for smaller quantities of high octane fuel or other refined products.

Above deck level, all access points to Holds 4 and 5 are intact and closed. Of course, the integrity of these holds must have been breached somewhere – or the ship would still be afloat. That damage appears to be out of sight and is likely to be on that part of the wreck which lies facing the sandy seabed. A swim along the decks reveals the most interesting array of fittings and other paraphernalia. The handrails are mostly intact and are as shallow as 12m on the upper starboard side. Alongside those on the port side is a large flexible fuel-transfer hose. Running along the centre of the deck are a number of raised metal tripod-like structures less than a metre high. These are connected along the top by a series of fuel pipes running to each of the cargo holds. All valves and hatches are shut tight.

There is a single mast complete as far as the crosstrees. This is encrusted with hard corals and rises up to a depth of 7m. Below the mast on the decks are a pair of cargo winches but no booms. Towards the stern of the ship, there is a small accommodation block with a number of firmly closed brass portholes. On the starboard side is a large doorway partially obscured by corals. Looking inside we could see part of the ship's Galley.

Behind this accommodation block, the rear deck itself is a confusion of ships fittings and items that look almost as though they don't really belong here. Raised above the deck, is the large gun platform. I had to be convinced that gun platforms were actually fitted to Tankers – but here is the proof. In every direction there is a great deal to see and explore. On both sides of the ship are large fire-hoses still tightly coiled as though waiting to be used. Alongside the port handrails, in addition to all the usual deck winches, bollards, cleats and other fittings, is a second fuel transfer hose.

Of even more interest, however, are the large open ventilation hatches which provide easy access to the engine room. No sooner had we entered this cavernous room, we were confronted by a prime example of a triple-expansion steam engine with an extra low pressure cylinder. I had never seen one quite like this before but I was well acquainted with standard 3 cylinder triples and this was pretty much the same – except for that extra cylinder.

Even though the ship is right over on her port side, light penetration is extremely good and I was able to find my way down to the next level quite easily. As I took even more photographs of the various components, I could see yet another level below revealing the ship's massive connecting rods.

Although quite tidy, the many features found within the engine room were either well rusted or covered in a layer of silt. The makers plate should still be bolted onto one of the bulkheads in there somewhere – something which will provide conclusive proof to satisfy anyone who may still be in doubt. Although I was generally preoccupied with photography, I did take time out for a good look around but nothing was immediately obvious. Back on the outside, there only remains a visit to the ship's beautifully rounded stern below which both the rudder and brass propeller are found half-buried in the sand at 28m.

POSTSCRIPT – Nobody can claim to know either the details or the fates of every ship that ever sailed through the Red Sea. From all the evidence

Looking aft along the deck of the *Turbo* with a capstan in the foreground.

I have carefully studied, I am happy to conclude that the half tanker at Râs Banas is very probably the *Turbo*. I use the word 'probably' only because of the absence of absolute conclusive proof. What is abundantly clear is that this is most definitely *not* the *Atlas* and any suggestion that the *Atlas* may also be found nearby is pure nonsense. Rightly identified or not, this is a great dive which provides something very different from all other wrecks found in this amazing part of the Red Sea. She also provides us with a tale of two shipwrecks for the price of one.

• Chapter XVIII •

Zealot & Maidan

Zealot
Lost off Daedalus Shoal 14 October 1876

Maidan
Lost off Rocky Island 10 June 1923

Unlike the other major shipwrecks detailed here, I have not visited either the *Zealot* or the *Maidan* simply because I was informed of their discovery only a few days before my final manuscript for this book was due at the publishers. Up to that point, I had been totally unaware of the existence of the *Zealot* and was only intending to include the briefest details of the *Maidan* (pronounced 'Mydarn') in the Appendix. This, however, all changed when, out of the blue, in November 2003 I received two separate unsolicited e-mails from divers who were completely unknown to me. Both were claiming to have discovered a previously unknown shipwreck.

The first e-mail arrived on 7 November and was from a German student called Markus Lohr. Markus informed me he had recently been diving off Daedalus Shoal and towards the end of his dive saw something far below and decided to take a quick look. What he found was a shipwreck, although he had no time to investigate. Two weeks later, however, he returned to the site and recovered a dinner plate. Whilst others scoffed at his claim of finding a wreck, he sent me photographs of that plate which bears the name *Helme Park – South Shields* within a belt surrounding a shipping company's flag.

Altogether, by this point in time, I had researched many hundreds of ships' names connected with the Red Sea and I had not previously heard of the *Helme Park*. I also had to consider the possibility that the dinner plate could have come from anywhere and might even be a hoax. Nevertheless, we certainly appeared to have a photograph of a genuine ship's plate. Furthermore, that plate was clearly very old and had spent some time underwater. In providing me with a photograph of something which appeared to be genuine *and* from a ship not easily traced, I was inclined to believe Mr Lohr was telling the truth and had found a shipwreck on Daedalus Shoal. It was Paul de Keijzer in Holland who tracked

the ship down and informed me it had been renamed *Zealot*. My own subsequent research revealed the *Zealot* was indeed lost on Daedalus Shoal in 1876. I was, therefore, happy to accept all that Markus Lohr had been kind enough to tell me and I am grateful to him for allowing me to reproduce his story here.

In the meantime, just three days later on 10 November, I received an e-mail from a Kimmo Hagman who informed me he and his friend Grant Searancke had also made an important discovery and were claiming to have found the wreck of the *Maidan*. Now just a minute! New shipwrecks are discovered once in a blue moon and within the space of 3 days, I was probably the only person to be aware of two such discoveries. I was now sceptical of both wrecks to say the least – especially as one well-known source had already claimed to have found the *Maidan* in 50m – and had even published photographs taken from the *Rosalie Moller* to support that false claim!

Consequently, I telephoned a few people and discovered Kimmo Hagman enjoys a high reputation as an underwater photographer. This was later confirmed when he sent me some extremely exciting photographs from a shipwreck I did not recognise. That said, there was still no actual proof they had found the *Maidan* and I made my scepticism very clear from the outset. I was then sent a short film of the wreck and discussed everything at great length with Brian Gilgeous – and Brian probably knows as much, if not more, about the *Maidan* as anyone.

So far, these were the facts of which I was aware; (1) The story of the *Maidan* and the circumstances surrounding her loss were already widely known to me and others. (2) The film and photographs show a substantial shipwreck in very deep water. (3) That shipwreck was completely unknown to me. (4) I identified the island shown in the background of the film as Rocky Island. (5) The stern of the ship shown in one particular photograph is very similar to that of the *Maidan*. (6) Nevertheless, there was no concrete proof to show that the wreck was the *Maidan*.

Despite the lack of concrete proof, it was evident that a new wreck had been found and I came to the conclusion it would be right and proper to believe Kimmo Hagman had found a very substantial shipwreck in the Egyptian Red Sea. Furthermore, from all the evidence provided, I was able to conclude that this new shipwreck is very probably the SS *Maidan*. For this reason, I am able to include the full details of this great ship instead of her being consigned to no more than a few lines – as was previously intended.

A WORD OF CAUTION – According to Markus Lohr, the wreck on Daedalus Shoal commences at 75m and goes down beyond that. Kimmo Hagman informs me the *Maidan* is between 90m and 120m. These wrecks are, therefore, far too deep for the average scuba diver visiting Egypt on holiday who might be tempted to take a casual look. These shipwrecks are, therefore of great interest to those technical divers who possess the appropriate qualifications, equipment, experience and skills and are included for that reason.

Zealot
(Approximate GPS: 24° 55·500N, 35° 50·500E)

DAEDALUS SHOAL – Daedalus Shoal is a small rocky outcrop that reaches the surface of the Egyptian Red Sea – almost in the middle of nowhere. The shoal is surrounded by very deep water on all sides. Whilst any number of unknown vessels may have foundered on this shoal, only two are recorded as being lost here – the other vessel being the SS *Dacca* (see Appendix).

THE SHIP – Officially described an 'iron spar-decked screw steamer,' the *Zealot* was built by John Readhead and Company of South Shields for William Wright, a ship owner from the same port. This general cargo vessel was launched in January 1873 as the *Helme Park*. Her dimensions were 74.85m x 9.53m with a draught of 3.25m and a displacement of 1,528 grt. She was fitted with a 2-cylinder compound inverted direct action steam engine built in Gateshead by Black, Hawthorn and Co. which provided 120 hp and a top speed of 12½ knots. The *Zealot* was owned and operated by John Glyn & Son and registered in Liverpool at the time of her loss.

Almost the entire history of John Readhead and Company of South Shields, England was lost during WW2. There are, therefore, no known photographs of the Zealot. This picture was compiled after extensive research by both the author and the artist and is regarded as accurate. (Rico Oldfield)

THE LOSS OF THE *ZEALOT* – On 26 September 1876 the *Zealot* left Liverpool with a cargo later described by the Board of Enquiry as 790 bales, 91 cases and 110 tons of iron valued at £24,700. She also carried two passengers and a crew of fifty-three, most of whom were Lascars. Her destination was Bombay and her Master Captain Joseph Best. According to the ship's log, it was an uneventful journey through the Mediterranean and the *Zealot* cleared Suez at 23.45 hrs on 12 October. By 01.56 hrs the following morning Shadwan Island was abeam at a distance of 2½ miles. Speed was increased to 12 knots and the master set a course of South 24° East on his standard compass. This was designed to take his ship four miles west of the Brothers Islands. The weather was clear and fine.

During the previous three years, Best had completed several lengthy journeys in this ship, having joined her when she was the *Helme Park*. Considered a hard task-master, he knew every single corner of his ship.

He was also meticulous. His verbal orders were always repeated in writing and these were then signed and acknowledged by each officer of the watch as they came on duty. At 06.15 hrs, 13 October, the light from Big Brother Island was first seen bearing 'Southeast one quarter degree South' and within an hour the lighthouse was clearly visible. At 08.20 hrs Best came on the bridge and, as was common practise, hauled up very close to the island in order to give himself the best possible 'exact fix' on his chart. He then set a course of South 34° East.

On paper, this course would appear to put the vessel almost directly onto Daedalus Shoal. Prevailing currents, however, were expected to place the vessel a full four or five miles further to the west during this leg of the journey. The day passed without incident but for some reason they did not make good time. This was put down to strong head currents – which were most unusual.

At midnight 13 October the second mate came on watch and took charge. The course, speed and conditions had remained unchanged. Best supervised the hand-over of duties and twenty minutes later retired to write his night orders. These included the instruction to call him at either 04.30 hrs or as soon as Daedalus Light came into view. These orders were read and signed by the second mate who also consulted the chart at the same time. Knowing the first mate would come on watch at 04.00 hrs, the second mate asked Best if there was any need for bearings to be taken at first light. Best repeated his instructions and said that the taking of any bearings should be left to him. At 04.00 hrs First Mate Jonathan Russell took over the watch and duly read and signed the night orders. The course still remained unchanged and everything was conducted in a businesslike manner. The second mate, however, had misgivings about their position and course and, having repeated what the

The Bollards on the stern of the *Zealot* at a depth of over 80m. (Kimmo Hagman)

master had said with regard to bearings, suggested the first mate take a closer look at the chart before he too retired.

Russell was not a particularly experienced First Officer, this being his first trip since being promoted to that status. He later testified at the formal Inquiry that he did call the master at 04.30 hrs at which time he said he informed Captain Best that Daedalus Light was not yet in sight. He said the master acknowledged this and instructed him to take an amplitude bearing at first light and call him again when Daedalus Light was seen.

At 05.15 hrs Russell was able to take that bearing before going into the chartroom to work on it. This took twenty minutes and when he returned to the bridge he immediately saw Daedalus Light almost dead ahead. Realising those twenty minutes had been crucial, Russell now appears to have been overcome with fear of retribution from his Captain. He later testified that he had acknowledged the lookout's call when the light was first reported, but said he had assumed it would have been much further away and continued to work on the chart. With the Helmsman located in a separate wheel-room from where he was unable to see out, everyone on board was wholly reliant on the officer of the watch for the safe navigation of their ship.

The *Zealot* was now in a position whereby she was still steaming at full speed and on collision course with Daedalus Reef. Russell, however, became intent on not drawing the master's attention to this predicament. Knowing that Best would 'feel' any sudden change in course, he ordered a very gradual series of changes of one degree south each time in order to miss the reef without revealing their plight to anyone. In this way, he felt he could also claim he was hauling up close to Daedalus in order to provide the master with the best possible 'exact fix.' Unfortunately, he lacked the experience necessary for such a series of complicated manoeuvres and, even though the ship continued to rapidly approach a very dangerous situation, he still made no attempt to either reduce speed or call the master.

Yet again he altered course by a further one degree but his efforts were making little difference to the ship, which maintained a top speed of 12 knots throughout. Then, in a last ditch attempt to do something more positive, he changed course a further five degrees south. That move, however, was far too little and far too late. At precisely 05.49 hrs, 14 October 1876 the *Zealot* struck Daedalus Shoal and bounced off. Russell immediately ordered the helm put hard over and the engines eased to slow. The master was on the bridge within moments.

Best later told the court he remembered being called but with Daedalus Light not yet in sight he felt his presence was not needed on the bridge until it *was* seen. He went on to say that, on arriving on the bridge, he saw Daedalus Light immediately off the port beam. Taking control of his

Divers inspect the propeller of the *Zealot* at a depth of over 85m. (Kimmo Hagman)

stricken ship, he stopped the engines and called all hands to prepare the boats. On sounding the wells, the ship was found to have over five feet (150cm) of water in the forward hold. The boats were immediately lowered and an orderly evacuation begun. At the same time, the ship was turned to face Daedalus with canvas being lashed under the hull in a bid to reduce the ingress of water. The ship's bow was then placed against the reef and some of the crew jumped ashore.

Having seen the two passengers and the majority of his crew safely evacuated, the Master then turned his attention to saving the ship. It was, however, already a lost battle and with the decks awash, Captain Best was the last to leave the *Zealot* which was then observed to go down by the stern and slide down the reef. Four hours later, after responding to a distress signal fired from the lighthouse, everyone was rescued by a passing French ship and taken to Suez. There were no casualties.

The following publications carried reports of the loss of the *Zealot*:

Lloyd's List dated 18 October 1876:
Casualty Report:
LIVERPOOL, 17th Oct 1p.m. – the *ZEALOT* hence to Bombay has been lost on Daedalus Reef, Red Sea; crew proceeded to Port Said; (above by telegram from Suez to the owners). Cargo consisted of 790 bales, 91 cases and 110 tons of iron; value £24,700.

Shipping and Mercantile Gazette dated 17 October 1876:
PORT SAID, Oct. 17, noon. (By telegraph): The *Zealot* (Steamer) from Liverpool for Bombay, has been totally lost on Daedalus. Crew taken off by French transport.

Shipping and Mercantile Gazette dated 19 October 1876:
Liverpool, Oct. 19, 11 a.m. (By telegraph): The *Zealot* (Steamer) from Liverpool for Bombay, before reported lost on Daedalus Reef, is sunk in 250 fathoms; no chance of saving cargo unless it floats out. (NB: 250 fathoms is 457m!)

Curiously, the House of Commons Parliamentary Papers for 1877 (Vol. 75) in which all vessels lost during the previous year are recorded, describes the *Zealot*'s cargo as coal. Clearly coal could never 'float out' from any wreck. Coal, however, is not mentioned anywhere else at all and appears to be entirely erroneous.

THE BOARD OF TRADE ENQUIRY – The formal Board of Trade investigation into the loss of the *Zealot* was held in Liverpool in November 1876. Having heard all the evidence given, the findings of the court were

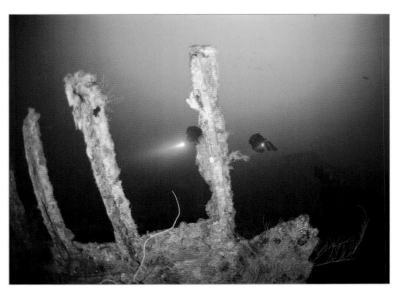

Two divers approach the damaged mid section of the *Zealot* at a depth of 75m. (Kimmo Hagman)

quite clear; 'We find the primary cause of the loss of the *Zealot* and her valuable cargo was due to the unskilful navigation of First Officer Russell who acted well beyond both his capabilities and authority in continuing to navigate the ship without seeking to inform the master when he first saw Daedalus Light as he had been instructed so to do.'

What is, perhaps, difficult to understand is that they also stated that 'Captain Best should have left more peremptory instructions to ensure his being on deck when Daedalus Light came into view.' I would have thought that instructions – given both verbally and in writing, would have been clear enough for anyone to follow. Nevertheless, as a result of their findings, the court suspended Russell's First Mate's Certificate for a period of twelve months and Best's Master's Certificate for six months.

DIVING THE *ZEALOT* – Markus Lohr's own account of having found this wreck is reproduced here. Markus was born in Ravensburg, Germany in 1978 and is currently studying intercultural business studies at the University of Passau. He first learned to dive in 1994 and in 1998 spent six months working in Egypt as a Dive Guide with the Red Sea Diving Centre. Since that time he has visited Egypt several times to work on safari boats and has amassed a very creditable 1600 dives. Markus is a CMAS 4 star diver and is also ANDI certified.

MARKUS LOHR'S DIVE – 'On 9 September 2003 we left the Brothers Islands and headed for Daedalus Shoal arriving at 06.30 hrs the following morning. Our first dive was an hour later where we were hoping to see the early morning Hammerhead Sharks but the weather thwarted our plan. The sea was too rough so we decided to dive on the sheltered side. I made a very deep dive and to my great surprise found myself looking at a shipwreck at a depth of 75m. It was well broken up but there was no doubt this was a ship. I swam along the wreck for a few moments but had still not seen the stern when I commenced my surfacing drills. Nobody else had seen the wreck. I realised it would be hard for others to believe, so I decided not to mention the wreck at all.

On 24 September, I returned to Daedalus but it was very difficult to pinpoint the wreck's exact position. On the second attempt, however, I found it straight away. This allowed me a little more time to explore the wreck. Even at 88m I still could not see the stern – although I could see two Admiralty Pattern anchors far below lying in the wreck. I also noticed something round. It was a dinner plate which I recovered from a depth of 92m.

A photograph of the dinner plate recovered by Markus Lohr from the wreck of the *Zealot*. It was from the insignia in the centre that Paul de Keijzer from Holland was able to positively identify the ship. (Marcus Lohr)

This is a wreck for Technical Divers with the appropriate qualifications, experience and equipment. The wreck itself is broken and I was unable to make out the bows. She is, nevertheless, a virgin shipwreck just waiting to be explored and all her secrets are lying down there with her – all of them. For the moment I shall keep her precise location to myself – at least until I am able to return.' (Markus Lohr)

POSTSCRIPT – Joseph Augustus Best was born in Plymouth in 1826 where he gained his Master's Certificate in 1856. His first command was the *Acastus* but ships with names beginning with the letter Z became something of a problem in later years. He was in command of the *Zampa* when she was lost in November 1866 and in command of the *Zigzag* which was lost the following August. He was given command of the *Helme Park* in October 1873 and remained with the ship when she changed owners in 1874 and became the *Zealot*. After losing his Master's Certificate for six months in November 1876, it was not until 1878 that he returned to sea. Having previously lost three ships he was probably finding it very difficult to secure a berth. Consequently, he completed very few trips between 1878 and 1882, did not go to sea in 1883 and after a single trip in the *Star* in 1884, appears to have retired.

Maidan

(Approximate GPS: 23° 36·00N, 36° 10·00E)

THE SHIP – Built by W. Hamilton & Co. of Glasgow, the *Maidan* was launched in March 1912. Officially described as a steel screw steamer, she was a large general cargo ship with dimensions of 152.4m (500 feet!) x 17.7m with a draught of 10m and a displacement of 8,205 grt. In 1919 she was fitted with a brand new 4 cylinder quadruple-expansion steam engine built by Messrs D. Rowan of Glasgow which was capable of producing 747 hp and a top speed of 12 knots (unladen). She was owned and operated by T & J Brocklebank of Glasgow, a shipping company much respected throughout the world and something of a legend in Liverpool. Captain Nicholas Breen was one of their most experienced and trusted employees and was given command of this magnificent ship in 1921. With the exception of the World War One years – a time when she was under the control of the Ministry of Transport, the *Maidan* was used exclusively on the eastern trade routes between Europe and India throughout her life.

THE LOSS OF THE *MAIDAN* – By 1923, Breen had already completed five lengthy journeys in the *Maidan* and there was no reason to suspect this would be any different. Indeed, it was an uneventful trip out and they duly arrived at Calcutta on 25 April where they were soon employed in replacing one cargo with another. The *Maidan* carried a crew of one hun-

dred, of whom eighty-three were Lascars. Breen was a man who made it his business to know every single detail of his ship and, if he had one fault, it was that he always knew best and would never take advice, no matter what the circumstances.

With the return cargo finally loaded and the hatches battened down for the long journey ahead, it was 22 May when Breen finally gave the order to slip the mooring lines as he rang down for Slow Ahead before edging out into the Ganges Delta towards the Bay of Bengal. Five days later they docked in what was then Ceylon and, after circumnavigating most of the Indian sub-continent, arrived in Bombay on 5 June. From here it was almost due east to the Gulf of Aden before they would finally enter the Red Sea. On 7 June, the *Maidan* arrived in Port Sudan for additional cargo and bunker coal and sailed from that port at 30 minutes past midnight on the morning of 9 June 1923.

It was from this point onwards that Breen began to make a number of uncharacteristic errors, almost as though he was suddenly deprived of all reason. According to the resultant Board of Trade enquiry, the weather was 'fine, clear and moderate' and the *Maidan* was maintaining a top speed of 10.5 knots. At 08.45 hrs bearings were taken from Abington Reef Beacon and at 09.45 hrs the course was altered to North 25° West True. Morning sights for longitude were obtained and later that day latitude was also determined. By this time, the ship's log showed they had travelled 118 miles from Port Sudan and at 16.15 hrs their course was altered once again. Breen later testified his intention was to pass five miles east of St. John's Island and use that island to obtain a definite fix.

At 18.45 hrs the first mate took bearings from the Elba Mountains which showed the *Maidan* to be 2½ miles west of her intended route.

The *Maidan* prior to World War I. (Scottish Maritime Museum)

A picture of the *Maidan* in the Suez Canal. This picture was found by the author amongst a pile of old postcards at a boot fair. (Unknown source)

Looking straight towards the stern of the *Maidan* which lies hard over on its port side showing the huge rudder below. (Kimmo Hagman)

This placed the ship much closer to the island but Breen insisted on leaving things as they were. In so doing, however, he failed to take into account the variable currents and other conditions peculiar to the Red Sea and his lack of action at this point was never justified. In short, there was nothing to be gained and much to be lost from sailing so close to an unlighted island in the dark. No further observations were then taken and at 23.30 hrs Breen, who had been on deck all day, retired to his cabin leaving orders to be called when St. John's Island was sighted. At 01.26 hrs 10 June, the Second Officer, who was in charge of the watch, suddenly sighted St John's – almost dead ahead, and estimated the distance as eight to ten miles. He immediately altered course one point to starboard and called the Captain, informing him of both the sighting and the action he had taken. Incredibly, at this crucial time, Breen appears to have been more intent on demonstrating how he had been right all along than in taking appropriate action. Despite it being quite clear the ship was nowhere near the intended course he had previously set and that the Second Officer's actions were insufficient to avert disaster, Breen did nothing!

With Breen being especially experienced in travelling the Red Sea, his actions remain wholly insupportable. Furthermore, even if they did clear the island, he knew that the much smaller and low-lying Rocky Island would then be dead ahead. With the open Red Sea off to starboard, it would have been the easiest thing in the world to change course, but this did not happen. Suddenly, discoloured water was seen off the port bow and the helm was immediately put hard-to-port and the engines full astern. According to the testimony of other officers on board, the vessel remained like this for a full four minutes before striking Rocky Island at 01.39 hrs, though with very little speed on the vessel when she did so. Soundings were taken and every attempt was made to back the vessel off but to no avail.

By daylight, different measures were being employed to stop the vessel's bottom from working the reef and these continued throughout the day. The *Maidan* was carrying a cargo of approximately 10,000 tons and seven passengers in addition to her crew. By 11.00 hrs the Lascars and the passengers were landed on the island and later that afternoon the *Warwickshire* came up and took them all on board. Yet later, when the *Maidan* was clearly in a dangerous condition, she also took on board the Master and remaining crew. At 19.10 hrs 10 June 1923, the *Maidan* slipped off the reef and sank in what was described as 'very deep water'.

PINPOINTING HER POSITION – Anyone who reads the Board of Trade report into the loss of the *Maidan* and compares the detailed comments to the appropriate Admiralty Chart, will be forgiven for becoming some-

The access hatch down to the engine room of the *Maidan* which has not been used since the ship sank in 1923. (Kimmo Hagman)

what confused. In the southern Egyptian Red Sea there is a large coral plateau called St. John's Reef. This, however, is not the St. John's Island mentioned in the report. It was only when I studied the Sailing Pilot for the Red Sea that I realised that Zabargad Island is also called St John's Island and in 1923 this was the name in common use. This revelation was further reinforced by Lloyd's List of 11 June 1923 which refers to Zabargad Island as Zebrejed Island as follows:

Lloyd's List dated 11 June 1923 (p.8 Col. 5):
Casualty Report:
SERIOUS ACCIDENT TO INDIAN LINER –
MAIDAN SINKING IN RED SEA
News of a serious shipping casualty in the Red Sea was received at Lloyd's yesterday. A cable from Port Sudan stated that the steamer *Maidan* owned by Messrs T. J. Brocklebank Ltd of Liverpool had reported by wireless at 2.30 am yesterday that she had gone ashore on Rocky Island off St. John's Island in the Red Sea. The forepeak and No. 1 Hold were flooded and the water had a depth of 9' in No. 2 Hold and was rising. Immediate salvage assistance was required. The *Maidan* was later reported to be in a sinking condition. A steamer 20 miles away was proceeding to her assistance.

The same issue of Lloyd's List then included the following additional information:

The *Maidan* was a Steel Screw Steamer of 8,205 tons and was built by Mess W. Hamilton & Co. at Port Glasgow in 1912. She left Calcutta on May 22 for London, Dundee and the Clyde and left Port Sudan on Saturday. During the first 2 years of the War the *Maidan* was used as an Army Transport. Rocky Island on which the *Maidan* struck is a small island about 3 miles south-eastward from St. John's or Zebrejed Island. St. John's Island is in Lat 23 36N Long 36 10E and lies 27 miles south-eastward from the southern point of the Râs Banas peninsula a prominent point on the western shore of the Red Sea. The two islands are about 250 miles from Port Sudan and 450 miles from Suez.

This information was quickly updated with news of the vessel's loss:

Looking up towards the rounded stern of the *Maidan* with her propeller and rudder in the foreground at a depth of over 100m. (Kimmo Hagman)

Lloyd's List dated 12 June 1923 (p.7 Col. 3):
Casualty Report:
Maidan – Port Sudan June 10. British Steamer *Maidan*: Master reports total loss; vessel sunk 8pm. Passengers and crew rescued, proceeding via steamer Warwickshire.

Alexandria June 11 – Steamer Morea reports steamer *Maidan* sunk seven yesterday evening off Rocky Island. Crew and passengers on Warwickshire.

Port Sudan June 11 – steamer *Maidan* – Master reports sunk in 100 Fathoms.

HOW THE *MAIDAN* WAS FOUND BY GRANT SEARANCKE – We wanted to put together a new wreck diving itinerary and asked Captain Nagy – skipper of the MV *Excel*, if he knew of any wrecks in the southern Egyptian Red Sea which were not dived. Captain Nagy was in charge of diving boats when the industry first began in Egypt and a fisherman before that. He told us how he had lost several anchors in one area off Rocky Island and had seen an image on the echo sounder which appeared to indicate a wreck in very deep water – although he couldn't be sure. I discussed everything with my good friend Kimmo Hagman who is a professional photographer and Dive Centre Manager of Colona Divers. We had long been intrigued by the story of the *Maidan* and agreed to take every opportunity to search for this wreck.

We began in May 2003 and after many fruitless searches and unsuccessful dives did not finally pinpoint her exact position until October. We had been looking in an area indicated by our captain and were at 60m when we saw wreckage far below us. Large air vents, cargo booms, wire and chain was scattered on the seabed. Then the bottom dropped away completely and we could no longer see anything except blue water all around us. It was clear we would need to use Trimix Closed Circuit Rebreather equipment to investigate this wreck further.

Over the following weeks I made a number of exploratory dives on Trimix 18/30 (18% oxygen, 30% helium, 42% Nitrogen) by myself. The first 2 attempts were unsuccessful because even at 70m there was no sign of the wreck. I then decided on one more attempt. On this occasion the current took me much further along the reef to a new area. Suddenly, on the seabed at about 80m I saw a ship's funnel and a large shadow in the distance. Eventually, I found myself above a huge wreck lying on its port side. I was at 72m and the wreck was at least another 20m below. The seabed itself was barely visible beyond that.

We were coming to the end of the 2003 season and it would be 5 months before we resumed our regular trips to Rocky Island. I was desperate to make a proper dive on the wreck and not merely hover from above, but could not find anyone to join me at such short notice. It was not until October 2003 when we finally dropped a 100m shot-line onto the wreck. I was using a twin set of Trimix 10/50 and decompression cylinders of Nitrox containing 65% oxygen (the highest I could manage).

Carrying my video camera, I descended the shot line. At 65m I could see nothing and became a little apprehensive. Then, at 70m, I saw a shadow stretching out below and suddenly the whole wreck opened up before me. At 82m I stood on top of the wreck. She was covered in large whip corals and red soft corals – all of which burst into rich colours when I switched on my video lights and began filming. At the stern, I descended to the seabed at 97m to film the large propeller and rudder. On reaching my planned dive limit of 10 mins at 100m, I began my ascent.

Back in Hurghada I showed Kimmo Hagman the video footage and his previously fully booked schedule was instantly pushed to one side as he joined me to explore the wreck further and take photographs. We made 2 dives – one to the stern and another to the bow which slopes away to over 120m. The following week Kimmo returned to the wreck and penetrated the engine room and cargo holds as far as 120m.
(Grant Searancke)

POSTSCRIPT 1 – Captain Nicholas Breen was born in Dublin in 1872 and gained his Master's Certificate in Belfast in 1903. On 18 December of that year he was given his first command – the *Harmodius*. He later went on to command *Gaekwar* from 1905 (re-named *Caernarvonshire* in 1906) and Cardiganshire from 1910. After completing a single journey on both the *Maidan* and *Matheran* as relief master, he was appointed to the *Anchoria* from 1912, *Manar* from 1917, *Mahronda* from 1919 and finally the *Maidan* from 1921. Altogether, Breen had now completed a total of thirty-four lengthy overseas journeys in addition to war duties and was one of the most experienced master mariners afloat.

In August 1923, the Board of Trade Enquiry found Captain Breen to have made serious errors of judgement on two counts: First, by not having sufficient regard to the variable currents in the Red Sea and by not altering course so as to give the unlighted islands of St John's and Rocky Island a wider berth and; Second, on being summoned to the bridge by the Second Officer, by not immediately altering course considerably more to starboard than it had already been altered by the Second Officer. For these serious errors of judgement the Court severely censured Captain Breen and, at the age of 51 years, it would appear he never went to sea again.

POSTSCRIPT 2 – One of the very first Territorial infantry battalions to be sent to France at the outbreak of World War One was the Liverpool Scottish Regiment who sailed from Southampton on 1 November 1914 on board the *Maidan*. By 1918 only sixty-five of the original 1,000 men were still serving with the Regiment in France, all the remainder having been either killed or wounded. These men became known as The *Maidan*ers and a silver salver called the *Maidan* Plate was presented to the Regiment to commemorate that historic journey.

The Regimental Museum website is at: www.liverpoolscottish.org.uk.

Appendix

Introduction

This Apppendix is divided into three parts:

Part One covers those reasonably well known dive sites which are best described as small, lesser-known wrecks which, because of their size, do not warrant a chapter in their own right. Each of these is an interesting site and makes an important contribution in its own way, either in terms of having become a natural extension to the adjacent reef or by providing a welcome change to existing diving programmes.

Part Two deals with ships' names and former names – both accurate and erroneous, which have been associated with the Red Sea for any reason. These vary from vessels which; are not yet found, are not even in the Egyptian waters, cannot be dived for any number of reasons and occasionally – never existed! As previously explained, considerable confusion surrounds many of Egypt's shipwrecks and one of the main reasons for this is the continued use of incorrect names. In some instances, ships' former names have been used in such a way as to suggest they belong to another, separate vessel altogether. My purpose here, therefore, is to remove as much of that confusion as possible.

Part Three is a list of ships lost in the Gulf of Suez and their last known position. The positions of other, unidentified wrecks, are also given. It should be noted, however, that, in addition to being a relatively narrow and extremely busy shipping route, the Gulf of Suez is also the centre of Egypt's oil industry. Many of these wrecks are, therefore, in areas which are strictly out-of-bounds to small craft and where anchoring, fishing and diving are strictly prohibited.

Whilst every attempt has been made to ensure these lists are complete and accurate, other names will very likely be added and I would be delighted to hear from anyone who would like to make a contribution.

Part One

Miscellaneous Minor Shipwrecks

ADAMANTIA K (unconfirmed GPS: 24° 12·551N, 35° 33·627E) – Known locally as the Half Wreck because the bows are apparently missing, this is the second of two vessels known to have foundered near Fury Shoal. A small freighter of 844 grt, she appears to have been owned by Mobil Oil (Nigeria) Ltd when lost. Lloyd's List dated 25 January 1958 carried the following item under their casualty report: '*Adamantia K* wrecked in vicinity of Hamata. Crew safe. Demands help… Vessel visible but Master declares not salvable.' Sometimes called *Hamada* (see below) or *Hamata* – being confused with either another wreck north of Fury Shoal or the name of the mountains near Marsa Sataya respectively.

AL KAHFAIN (GPS: 26° 39·572N, 034° 6·507E) – Former Liverpool-Belfast passenger/vehicle ferry Ulster Queen. On 1 November 2005, just as she had commenced a journey from Hurghada to Jeddah, fire broke out in the engine room and 58 crew members were rescued. The ship was then taken in tow for Safaga but sank some 4 miles later. There were no casualties. Little is known about the state of this wreck which is believed to be unstable and, therefore, dangerous.

AL-QAMAR AL-SAUDI AL-MISRI (*The Moon of Saudi and Egypt*) –. Originally built for DFDS Seaways, Denmark as the *Trekroner*, this 125m Egyptian twin-screw roro passenger/vehicle ferry of 7,697 grt was built in Italy and completed in 1970. In May 1994 she departed Jeddah with over 1,000 passengers and a crew of 63. At Safaga some 500 passengers disembarked leaving 527 passengers and crew on board for the final leg of the journey to Suez. At approximately 2330 hours on 18 May 1994 one of the ship's boilers exploded and fire quickly engulfed the ship. The ship drifted for some considerable distance before finally sinking in the early hours of 19 May between Shadwan Island, Sha'ab el Erg and

There are no known photographs of the *Tien Hsing*. This photograph is of a type of Tugboat that is very similar. (World Ship Society)

390. TREKRONER 1970-1971
DANA CORONA (I) 1971-1979 / DANA SIRENA (II) 1979-1983

Twin screw passenger and car ferry, 3 decks • 7697gt, 3890nt, 1008dw, 1971: 7672gt, 3669nt, 1021dw • 124.85/108.59x19.31/19.25x12.02/5.21 • Cantieri Navali del Tirreno e Riuniti S.p.A., Riva Trigoso, no.281 • 2D 2SA 2x12cyl. (420x900), type B&W 1242-VT2BF-90, 12000bhp, 21kn., by the builder at their Ancona works • Passengers: 204 I, 250 II, 718 total, 1971: 622. Cars: 120.

Taken from an old DFDS Seaways brochure showing the *Al-Qamar Al-Saudi Al-Misri* sailing under her original livery as the *Trekroner*. (DFDS Seaways)

Siyul. Twenty one passengers were lost in this tragedy which came just 2½ years after the loss of the *Salem Express* and only 7 weeks after this ship had previously run aground near Safaga. On 20 August 2007, the wreck of the *Al-Qamar Al-Saudi Al-Misri* was discovered by Aaron Bruce and Paul Vinten of Emperor Divers, Egypt a considerable distance from her last stated position. They reported the wreck as being on her starboard side at a depth of 65m to the uppermost port side and 85m to the seabed.

THE BARGE AT BLUFF POINT (GPS: 27° 40·679N, 33° 48·276E) – My pet name for this small barge is The Eggshell. She lies in the bay immediately south of Bluff Point. Numerous opinions have been published suggesting various origins of this vessel, including; Egyptian Navy vessel sunk during the Six-day war and later salvaged; a barge called *Sea Breeze* lost in tow during a storm; a diving boat and even a cruising yacht. I favour the barge theory.

At night this is an outstanding dive site. Comprising an open hull with no decking or superstructure whatsoever, she lies, like a broken eggshell, on the seabed. Her dimensions are approximately 30m x 6m and she is covered in hard and soft corals with a pair of very large Giant Moray Eels permanently in residence. For some reason, this vessel attracts spectacular fish life and the large numbers of Lionfish are particularly photogenic. During daylight hours there is often a large Turtle seen nearby. Sadly,

too many boats are dragging their anchors right through the delicate wreckage and she is not likely to survive for much longer.

BELINA (GPS: 27° 10·695N, 033° 49.929E). I am informed this former safari boat sank in 1999 after having caught fire. There were no casualties. Located opposite the Marine Sports Club, Hurghada, this steel hulled wreck lies in 9m of water with her upper parts just breaking the surface. Approx 50m in length she sits upright with a slight list to starboard. Particularly good for macro-photography (especially Nudibranchs) although a visit to this wreck will also include; Barracuda, Batfish and Boxfish.

THE BRICK WRECK (GPS 27° 47·767N, 33° 51·334E) – This wreck is clearly marked on Admiralty Chart 2375 and has been erroneously named *Carina* – after the name of a café in Hurghada! Despite concentrated efforts to formally identify this wreck, she remains unidentified. An interesting vessel, this was once a substantial sail & steam vessel circa 1870-1900. Wreckage comprises an extensive, shallow debris field on the northwest corner of Sha'ab Danaba which is immediately north of Shag Rock at Sha'ab Ali. Items of interest include 5 large boilers, bow and stern sections covered in well-established corals. According to the UK Hydrographic Office, the cargo is reported to have included bricks.

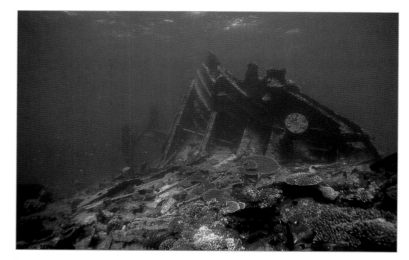

The view towards the stern of the Brick Wreck. Note the huge propeller shaft.

EL QAHER – Former British Zambezi class Destroyer leader built by Vickers Armstrong, Newcastle and completed as HMS *Myngs* (RO6) on 31 May 1943. Her dimensions were 103.5m x 11m with a draught of

Colourful soft coral growth is found on the remains of
one of the *Jolanda*'s containers.

4.9m (full load) and a displacement of 1,710 grt. Her original armament comprised; Four 4.5 in, two 2 pdr, three 40 mm and two 20 mm guns plus eight 21 in. torpedo tubes. Named after the Admiral and Pirate Sir Christopher Myngs (1625-1666), this ship was one of two similar vessels sold to the Egyptian Navy in May 1955 (the other being HMS *Zenith*). Renamed *El Qaher*, she was modernised prior to delivery and later re-fitted during 1963-4 at which time her torpedo tubes were removed and her mast altered. On 16 May 1970, Israeli jet aircraft sank the *El Qaher* near Port Berenice. It would appear that Ahmed Fadel, a senior dive guide with Emperor Divers was amongst the first to dive this wreck. First indications are that part of the foredeck and superstructure, including the leading guns, are out of the water. The remainder of this shallow-draught vessel are found on a ledge, apparently held in place by the star-board anchor. Below the surface, there is much evidence of damage and an heroic defence of the ship before she was finally sunk.

ENDYMION – 16m yacht owned by Australian Anthony Corbyn lost in October 1998 after navigational error. A published report by the divers who found this wreck stated she was lying on her starboard side at a max-imum depth of 15m but they did not reveal her position.

EXCALIBUR (GPS: 27° 13·560N, 33° 50·814E) – Little is known about why this charter yacht sank at her mooring, close to the Egyptian minesweeper *Miniya* (Chapter 13). Currents can be quite strong and some divers pre-fer to drift past both vessels in a single dive. This is also a shore-dive but beware of surface traffic. A classic vessel in her day, there is still much to see and explore before all the woodwork finally succumbs to the inevitable ravages of the sea.

FISHING BOAT – Nothing is known of this fishing boat, sunk on the southern side of Mikauwa Island which lies close to St. John's Reef. The wreck is both intact and perfectly upright at a depth of 50m on a muddy seabed. The stern rests against a sandy slope. The boat's framework reaches up to within 33m of the surface. There is evidence of attempts to lift the wreck with various bits of lifting gear still attached to the boat and more strewn over the seabed. A very good dive, though visibility is very poor.

HADIA – Possible identity of the small shipwreck known locally as the Plastic Wreck on account of the cargo she was carrying. One of two ves-sels known to have foundered south of Fury Shoal, the *Hadia* was built in 1949 and lost after 1970 (date unknown). Sometimes called *Hamada* or *Hamata*, these names having been confused with either the Hamata mountains or the following vessel.

HAMADA (last known position: GPS: 24° 26·300N, 35°12·787E) – Cypriot freighter lost on 28 June 1993 north of Fury Shoal. Built by J. Lewis & Sons of Aberdeen, she displaced 499 grt and had two cargo holds forward of bridge and engine room aft. The *Hamada* was powered by a 7-cylinder diesel engine built by British Polar Engines Ltd of Glasgow. The loss of this ship was attributed to an error in navigation. Her name is often confused with the Hamata mountains.

HEBAT ALLAH (GPS: 27° 09·281N, 33° 56·973E) – Little is known of this vessel which is apparently a 300 tonne former freighter some 51m in length. The author is informed that the vessel was delibvertely sunk by local dive operators in August 2004 in a bid to reduce the pressure on local reefs. According to a report by Martyn Farr, the vessel sits upright on a even keel where it is 45m to the seabed and 27m to the top of her masts.

JOLANDA (pronounced Yolanda) – Cypriot registered freighter built by SA Juliana Construction Gijonesa of Gijon and launched in 1964. Her dimensions were 74.8m x 10.75m with a draught of 3.5m and a displacement of 1,153 grt. Her diesel engines were built by Masch Augsburg of Nürnberg and her last owners were Seabrother Marine Co. Ltd of Piraeus, Greece. Lloyd's Register of Shipping 1979/1980 describes this ship as a motor fishing vessel although she was carrying containerised cargo when lost.

On 1 April 1980 the *Jolanda* struck a reef near Râs Mohammed and came to rest on her port side in shallow water balanced precariously above a very steep drop-off. In July/August 1986, British diver and author Lawson Wood took his family to Egypt intent on showing his children this particular shipwreck. As they approached the site, however, the sea became far too rough and they were unable to locate the mooring line attached to the wreck. Consequently, they moored on the lee side of Shark Observatory. That night, there was a particularly violent storm and the *Jolanda* slipped off the reef into very deep water. Lawson and his two children had a very narrow escape. The remains of containers which were being carried as deck cargo – complete with their contents of bathroom fittings, a number of deck hatches from the ship itself and a crushed BMW motor car are still found above the reef. Over time, the site has become known as Yolanda Reef – named after the wreck, but spelt incorrectly. The ship itself has now been discovered at a depth of 205m.

LARA (GPS 28° 00·717N, 34° 28·433E) – Cypriot freighter of 4,752 grt built in Germany and launched in 1956. In November 1982 the *Lara* drove hard onto Jackson Reef in the Straits of Tiran where her wreckage is found today. Popular legend has it that the accident was an insurance fraud after it was discovered there was only sufficient fuel on board to reach the reef on which she foundered. Curiously, it is also alleged that somebody remained on board the stricken vessel until 1985 giving rise to further allegations in connection with drug trafficking. It is also said that the Egyptian authorities ordered the ship demolished.

The first time I saw the *Lara* was in 2000 by which time the rear half of the ship was gone and what remained was nothing more than a section of large and somewhat square-shaped framework. It was immediately obvious to me that the elements would not have reduced the vessel to such a shape. With Paolo Guiotto of TGI Sinai, I went to investigate the seabed below the wreck. What we found was quite incredible and for some weeks we wrongly thought we had discovered a new wreck altogether.

Eventually, however, we realised that we were looking at the rest of the *Lara*. Large sections of this ship have been cut away and literally dropped over the side of the reef coming to rest in 50-60m of water. At one point, there is a complete cross-section from the bridge all the way down to the keel – looking as though a giant knife had cut through the ship. Elsewhere are other sections including a large part of the keel running all the way to the propeller. A fascinating dive and one where we were accompanied by a turtle almost throughout.

OIL RIG – A short distance north of Bluff Point on Gobal Sheghir, is part of an Oil Rig unit which appears to have been lost whilst being towed either from or to the Ashrafi Oilfields. Parts of the unit protrude from the sea making this a very shallow dive which is hard to recommend.

SOMAYA II – The loss of this dive charter boat alleges that her skipper placed his vessel on the leeward side of Sha'ab Shear and ran out two mooring lines to the reef and one astern. During the night the wind changed and the stern line broke putting the vessel straight onto the reef. There is not much to see with all the superstructure and engines having been removed. This is a popular mooring site and the vessel may have limited interest as a night dive. Being wooden, she will not last very long.

TANK SITE (GPS 27° 51·076N, 34° 17·475E) – It is said that, prior to handing the Sinai Peninsula back to Egypt under the terms of the Camp David Agreement, Israeli armed forces dumped a number of tracked vehicles and small lorries over the cliff rather than take them back to Israel. The tracked vehicles appear to be very similar in design to WW2 vintage Bren Carriers. There are no 'tanks' here but tracked vehicles are frequently confused with tanks, hence the name of this site. An interesting collection of vehicle which litter the steep slope down to about 28m.

TIEN HSING – Whilst the Royal Navy Museum, Portsmouth and the book by Bill Hannan, *Fifty Years of Naval Tugs* have confirmed the identity of this wreck, a dedicated and extremely competent research group from Holland have expressed doubts. Any further details about this particular vessel would, therefore, be welcomed. In the meantime, the limited information available to me is as follows. The *Tien Hsing* was a harbour tugboat of 268 grt built by Ta Chung Hua of Shanghai and completed in 1935. She was then requisitioned by the British Admiralty in 1941 for coastal service duties and later foundered during a passage from Suez to Massawa on 26 October 1943. Known locally as The Tugboat at Abu Galawa, she has also been called the *Tienstin* and *Tiensin*. This is a fabulous little wreck. The bows are wedged firmly onto a shallow reef and just break the surface. The stern rests on the sandy seabed at 18m, creating a swim-through beneath the keel. With a significant list to starboard, the entire port hull is covered in an incredible array of hard corals. From the foredeck, the diver can drop down into the open hold and swim underneath the wheelhouse and into the engine room. The triple-expansion steam engine is still intact. Elsewhere brass portholes can still be seen. Above the engine, an exit allows the diver to continue on and explore the typically rounded stern. Propeller and rudder are partly embedded in the sand and, moving back to the reef on the port side, the anchor is found – also embedded in the sand, with the chain running all the way up to the hawse-pipe. This is an outstanding night dive.

TUGBOAT AT SHARM EL SHEIKH – Nothing is known of this 30m firefighting harbour tugboat which, apparently, lies at a depth of 18-20m within an area of the harbour called Sharm El Moiya. The wreck is reputedly intact and attracts some interesting marine life.

TURKIA – Nothing is known of this wreck. Claimed to have been discovered in 2007 sitting upright in a depth of 24m and located some 150 miles north of Sha'ab Ali, by my reckoning, this places the wreck a few miles south of the port of Suez. This shipwreck may, therefore, be in an out-of-bounds location.

ZABARGAD FREIGHTER – This substantial shipwreck is found inside a lagoon on the eastern side of Zabargad Island just south of the jetty. First reported by Hans Hass in the 1950s, she is thought to be of Russian origin. The wreck has been featured in various magazine articles and at least one book. Despite extensive research, however, I am still unable to identify this vessel. I am informed, she is over 70m long, probably displaced something in the region of 2-3,000 grt and was probably engaged in re-supplying the military outpost on Zabargad Island when she became lost. My original intention was to identify this wreck and feature the vessel as one of the main chapters in this book. Consequently, in August 2002, we embarked on a serious mission to undertake a thorough inspection of the wreck in order to unearth whatever clues might exist. Sixteen divers were arranged in groups of four with each group being given a specific area to search and investigate. Just as we arrived at Zabargad Island, however, our skipper was informed by radio that the wreck had been placed out-of-bounds until further notice by the Egyptian authorities. It would be very wrong of me 'not' to mention the fact that any particular shipwreck or other dive site was out-of-bounds. There exists a number of offshore marine parks throughout the Egyptian Red Sea where visiting divers are required to pay a fee before being allowed to dive. One such marine park is located on the western side of Zabargad Island. Our freighter, however, is on the eastern side and is, therefore, outside the park's boundaries. Divers who have paid their fees and obtained permission to dive Zabargad Island marine park, do NOT have permission to dive this wreck. The military outpost on Zabargad Island is still manned and I would caution any diver against visiting this wreck without first obtaining very specific permission – in writing! For the meantime, I would be delighted to hear from anyone with further information about this wreck.

ZABARGAD TUGBOAT – A short distance from the unidentified freighter at Zabargad Island is a small vessel which appears to be a tugboat and which also came to grief many years ago. Once again, specific details are not known although it is likely she was also engaged in re-supplying the military outpost when lost. This vessel is also out-of-bounds.

PART TWO

Miscellaneous Ships and Names

ABOUDY – Nothing is known of this vessel reported as being a 75m Egyptian cargo ship said to have foundered off Râs Gharib in 1988. This vessel may have been confused with the *Talita*.

ADAMASTOS – Former name of the *Zingara*.

AFRICA – Former name of the *Tirrenia*.

AFRODITI H – Former name of the *Hamada*

AGHIA BARBARA – Incorrect name given to the *Agia Varvara*.

AGHIOS LEFTERIS – Former name of the *Lara*.

AIDA II – Incorrect name given to the *Aida* wrecked on Big Brother Island.

ALA EDDIN – Former name of the *AL KAHFAIN*.

ALASKA II – Greek general cargo vessel built at Santander and launched in 1959. Her dimensions were 82m x 12.32m with a draught of 7.01m and a displacement of 1,012 grt. On 8 April 1986, during a journey from Jeddah to Suez in ballast, this ship sustained an explosion in her engine room and sank within 10 minutes at position 26° 15'N, 34° 28'E. Two crew were lost and the remaining nine were rescued after 10 hours adrift.

ALITA – Incorrect name given to the *Talita*.

AL KAHERA – Former name of the *AL KAHFAIN*

ALLAGUASH – Former name of the *Tirrenia*.

AL-QAMAR AL-SAUDI II (1983-1987) & Al Qamar Al Saudi (from 1988). – Former names of the *Al-Qamar Al-Saudi Al-Misri*.

AL-SALAM BOCCACCIO 98 – Panamanian registered roro ferry measuring 118m (387 ft) in length and displacing 11,779 grt. Built in Naples in 1970, this vessel was previously operated by the Tirrenia Maritime Company and used in the Mediterranean until sold to El Salam Maritime Transport Company of Cairo in 1998. Renamed *Al-Salam Boccaccio 98*, she was primarily intended for use on the Mecca pilgrim trade between various Egyptian ports and Jeddah. To this end, she underwent extensive structural alterations above deck level to provide further accommodation which increased her carrying capacity to 1,487 passengers and crew. It was thought by some that this additional weight so high up on the ship might have made the vessel somewhat "top-heavy." Nevertheless, the ship was inspected twice in 2005 with no serious problems being reported. On 2 February 2006, the Al-Salam Boccaccio 98 departed the Saudi Arabian port of Duba for Safaga - a distance of 120 nautical miles. Officially, she was carrying 1,305 passengers, 96 crew, 16 lorries and 22 cars.

The ship was later reported to have sunk some 40 miles from her destination with great loss of life. Throughout the days immediately following this disaster, there were many confusing and conflicting reports. Some stated that no distress signal was sent but others insisted otherwise. RAF Kinloss, however, picked up an automated distress signal at 2358 hrs on 2 February. This signal was of type which is automatically activated on contact with water - indicating the ship was already sunk by this time.

Survivors told how a fire had broken out shortly after the boat had left Duba but that Captain Sayed Omar chose not to return to port but continue on to Safaga. Some stated the fire started in one of the lorries whereas others said it started in a luggage area and spread to the engine room. It was also reported that, although the fire alarm was initially sounded, the Captain later informed passengers that the fire had been extinguished and that it was safe to remove all lifejackets...

The large amounts of seawater used to fight the fire, however, were later stated as causing a loss of stability in the vessel itself. It was said that this additional water sloshing about inside the ship caused a severe list over to port - from which the ship never recovered. This situation may have been made worse by the weight of the additional accommodation built above deck level. In any event, the Al-Salam Boccaccio 98 disappeared from radar screens just before midnight on 2 February 2006 with the loss of over 1,000 lives - all but a few of whom were Egyptians. Captain Sayed Omar was a 1965 graduate of the Egyptian Naval Academy, gained his Master's certificate in 1972 and joined the El Salam Maritime Transport Company in 1998. Whilst Captain Omar is alleged to have left the sinking ship and taken to a lifeboat with some of his fellow ships' officers, he does not appear to have survived.

AL TAHRA – Former name of the *Salem Express*.

AMINAH II – Saudi Arabian general cargo vessel built in Nantes and launched in 1956. Her dimensions were 69.3m x 11.26m with a draught of 5.95m and a displacement of 1,194 grt. On 8 June 1980 the entire crew of *Aminah II* were rescued by a ship with one of the longest names in Maritime history – the *Fliegerkosmonaut der DDR Sigmund Jahn*. The *Aminah II* had been drifting for four days and sank soon after being abandoned at position 17° 23'N, 40° 33'E.

AN ANNE – Liberian registered bulk carrier built in Glasgow and launched in 1962. Her dimensions were 152.6m x 20.43m with a draught of 11.89m and a displacement of 9,894 grt. With a cargo of Rock Phosphate, the *An Anne* departed Aqaba for Karachi and on 20 February 1983 struck Abu Faramish Reef about 35 miles north of Jeddah. The vessel subsequently broke in two before sinking.

ANATOLI – Cypriot general cargo vessel built in Germany and launched in 1953. Her dimensions were 94.77m x 13.67m with a draught of 8.31m and a displacement of 2,769 grt. The Anatoli had been at anchor off Jeddah since 30 October 1976 awaiting a cargo when, on 28 November, the American steam barge carrier *Lash Atlantico* collided with her. The *Anatoli* sank at position 21° 27' 48"N, 39° 07' 12"E.

ANGELA – Former name of the *Kimon M*.

ANNA B – Former name of the *Chrisoula K*.

ANTONIA – Original name of the *Loullia*.

ANTONIOS III – Lebanese steamship built in New Orleans and launched in 1944. Her dimensions were 79.23m x 12.88m with a draught of 6.21m and a displacement of 1,598 grt. On 5 March 1966, the *Antonios III* ran hard aground north of Port Sudan at position. 21° 15'N, 37° 12'E. The vessel was abandoned as a constructive total loss.

ARCHON MICHAEL – Panamanian registered freighter of 4,809 grt. On 18 December 1962 whilst at anchor off Abu Zanimah in the Gulf of Suez, the *Archon Michael* dragged her anchors in strong winds and was lost.

ATHENIA – Former name of the *Agia Varvara*.

ASLAN – Turkish troopship built by Barclay Curle & Co and completed in 1872. Her dimensions were 106.8m x 11.2m with a draught of 8.4m and a displacement of 2,541 grt. On 1 April 1901, the Aslan was wrecked near Yenbo with the loss of approx. 180 lives.

ATLANTIC TRADER 1 – See *Marko Tasilo*.

ATLAS – See Chapter 17.

ATTIKI – Greek general cargo vessel of 3,320 grt built by Imabari Zosen of Japan and launched in 1966. On 24 April 1978, during a voyage from Genoa to Port Sudan with a cargo of cement, the *Attiki* ran hard aground near Râs Shukier at position 27° 59' 34"N,

33° 28' 36"E and was abandoned as a constructive total loss. The following month a fire broke out gutting much of the vessel.

AVOCET (1) – Original name of the *Hamada* (lost 28 June 1993).

AVOCET (2) – British freighter wrecked at Hodeidah in March 1887 after striking an unmarked reef.

AVRA – Greek freighter of 988 grt launched in 1943. On a journey from Suez to Gizan with a cargo of 1,350 tons of cement, the *Avra* sank in position 24° 50'N, 35° 16'E. The loss was caused by structural failure of the ship during bad weather. All the crew were saved.

AYA VARVARA & AYIA VARVARA – Incorrect names given to the Agia Varvara on account of her name being pronounced with a silent 'g'.

BACCHIS – Cypriot freighter of 2,494 grt built in Bremerhaven and launched in 1950. On 9 August 1977, during a voyage from Greece to Saudi Arabia with a cargo of bagged cement, the *Bacchis* ran aground on Sha'ab Ashrafi. Badly holed, the engine room and holds flooded and the cargo solidified. The vessel was abandoned as a constructive total loss. This wreck is marked on Admiralty Chart 2375 at position 27° 49' 09"N, 35° 39' 18"E. In July 2002, mainmast and bows were seen above the surface – but the remainder of this vessel is now and extensive debris field in shallow water.

BAHIA BLANCA – Original name of the *Umbria*.

BAKR – Egyptian motor survey vessel of 416 grt built in Kiev and launched in 1964. On 14 October 1973, during the Yom Kippur War, the *Bakr* was attacked by Israeli missiles and sunk off Râs Gharib.

BASTION – Russian refrigerated ship damaged by mine in the Southern Red Sea on 6 August 1984. The vessel continued with its journey – no reported casualties.

BELKIS I – Saudi Arabian roro/general cargo vessel damaged by mine in Gulf of Suez on 20 September 1984. The vessel continued with its journey – no reported casualties.

BELMORE – Small cargo boat of 168 grt. On 18 June 1908, during a voyage from the Clyde to Sydney with a general cargo, the *Belmore* was lost at Râs Gharib in the Gulf of Suez. Reported tonnage for this vessel seems remarkably small for such a journey.

BIG ORANGE XII – Panamanian well-stimulating vessel damaged by mine in Gulf of Suez on 28 July 1984. The vessel continued with its journey – no reported casualties.

BIRTE JENSEN – Former name of the *Tirrenia*.

BITO – Former name of the *Gladys Moller*.

BLUE BELL – Incorrect name given to the *Blue Belt*.

BLUE BELT – Saudi Arabian general cargo vessel of 2,399 grt built by Howaldts-werke A. G. of Hamburg and launched in 1950. On 2 December 1977, during a journey from Jeddah to Port Sudan with a cargo of 181 cars, 6 trucks, various trailers and spares, the *Blue Belt* struck Sha'ab Suadi Reef 50 miles north of Port Sudan. All the Crew were safely rescued and on 5 December the ship slipped off the Reef and sank.

BLUE SEA – Saudi Arabian motor passenger vessel of 11,440 grt built in La Spezia and launched as the Lloyd Triestino passenger liner *Europa* in 1952. On 12 November 1976 this ship was berthed at Jeddah when fire broke out. Many hundreds of pilgrims escaped unhurt before the *Blue Sea* was towed out of port and anchored at position 21° 29' 55"N, 39° 07' 08"E – where she subsequently sank.

BOLA NO 1 – Panamanian freighter of 8,603 grt built by Uddevallavarvet A/B of Sweden and launched in 1956. On 2 June 1979, during a journey from Aqaba to India with a cargo of 10,300 tonnes of phosphates, the Bola No 1 struck a rock in the south of the Gulf of Suez and later sank at position 27° 45'N, 34° 54'E. All 27 crew were rescued.

BOLESLAW KRZYWOUSTY – Polish freighter of 8,146 grt built in 1970. On 3 January 1990 the *Boleslaw Krzywousty* was attacked from the Eritrean shore by rocket fire. The ship subsequently sank 600 miles from Massawa at GPS position 16° 23·5N, 39° 12·2E.

Twenty-nine crew and the wife of one ship's officer were all captured by Eritrean rebels but later released. Vessel was subsequently declared a war constructive total loss.

BOREALIS – Cypriot freighter of 941 grt built in 1960. On 1 October 1976, during a voyage from Haql for Limassol in ballast, the *Borealis* ran aground off Maqna in the Gulf of Aqaba and was abandoned as a constructive total loss.

BOSNIA – Original name of the *Frangestan*.

BRITISH LANTERN – Former name of the *OLIGARCH*

BRUNSBÜTTEL – Original name of the *Kimon M*.

CAPE CLEAR – British freighter of 5,085 grt lost after a collision with the Henry Dearborn (US) near Suez on 21 August 1944. Due to war-time restrictions in force at the time, little information was made available about this wreck. She is, however, thought to be lying at position 28° 22'N, 33° 12'E.

CARLISLE – Name given to spurious claim of a new shipwreck said to be a Hospital ship found somewhere north of the *Thistlegorm*. If indeed any such wreck exists, the name appears to have been confused with that of HMS *Carlisle*.

HMS CARLISLE – British Anti-Aircraft Cruiser of 4,190 tons converted from a Light Cruiser in 1938. She was built by Fairfield and Co. and launched in 1918. This ship escorted convoys into the Red Sea and was on hand to rescue survivors when the *Thistlegorm* was bombed in 1941. She later joined the Mediterranean Fleet. On 9 October 1943, in company with four Destroyers, she made a sweep of the Scarpanto Straits off the coast of Rhodes at a time when German troops were reinforcing the Greek islands. The ships became the target for a full scale attack by German aircraft – mainly dive-bombers, and the *Carlisle* was badly damaged and disabled. HMS *Carlisle* sank later that day. Any suggestion that this ship is now found in the Red Sea is fallacious.

CEDAR PRIDE – Lebanese freighter of 1,161 grt built in Gijon and launched in 1964. On 2 August 1982, she was in ballast at the port of Aqaba when a fire broke out sustaining extensive damage to the engine room and accommodation. The Captain and Cook were killed. The vessel was later declared a constructive total loss but remained in port for over three more years before being deliberately sunk at position 29° 31' 30"N, 34° 59' 30"E – as an artificial reef and diving attraction.

CEDAR STAR – Lebanese freighter of 1,315 grt built in 1961. On 22 November 1978, during a voyage from Lebanon to Port Sudan carrying 170 soldiers of the Arab League Peace Keeping Force, the Cedar Star ran aground on Elba Reef in Sudanese waters. Due to high seas and the vessel's precarious condition, it was a full three days before Sudanese military

The *Cedar Star*. (World Ship Society)

helicopters were able to rescue passengers and crew. The vessel was then abandoned as a constructive total loss. This very interesting wreck is approx. 21 hours sailing time from Port Sudan.

CENTURION – Former name of the *Gladys Moller*.

C. EREGLI – Turkish bulk carrier of 9,271 grt built in 1974. Following a collision with the 81,000 tonne tanker *Mendana Spirit* off the coast of Yemen on 10 February 1991, the C. Eregli sank with the loss of one life – the Captain.

CESARE BATTISTI – Italian Navy Destroyer built in 1926. Her dimensions were 90.1m x 9.3m with a draught of 3.2m and a displacement of 1,058 grt. On 4 April 1941, the *Cesare Battisti* was sunk by British destroyers off Massawa. Her normal complement was 142.

CHIEH LUNG – Panamanian freighter of 6,629 grt built in 1953. On 16 January 1979, while in an empty condition at Hodeidah Roads, the *Chieh Lung* dragged her anchor and then drifted for 10 miles before eventually becoming wrecked.

CIUDAD DE CUCUTA – Former name of the *Kimon M*.

COLONA IV – One of the early safari boats operating in the Red Sea. Apparently, lost in a storm in 1995 and now resides at a depth of 75m off Hurghada.

CREST LION – Former name of the *Lara*.

CRISTOBAL – Panamanian motor tanker of 3,250 grt built in 1945. On 23 February 1967, the *Cristobal* sank off the Morgan 2 oil well in the Gulf of Suez at position 28° 09' 56"N, 33° 25' 59"E after water had flooded her engine room. She was carrying oil samples for analysis at the time and her entire crew were safely rescued.

CROWN OF GALICIA – Original name of the *Gladys Moller*.

DACCA – (I am indebted to Dr Carson Dron of Australia for information regarding this ship. Dr Dron's grandparents were passengers on board the SS *Dacca* at the time of her loss and, after being safely rescued, finally arrived in Mackay, Australia on board the SS *Taroba*.) The *Dacca* was a British steel screw steamship of 3,908 grt built in Lanark, launched in 1882, registered in Glasgow and officially described as a passenger cargo ship. Operated by the British India Associated Steamers, she was brigantine-rigged and fitted with two engines. The *Dacca* was used exclusively between Great Britain and either India, China or Australia throughout her life. At 0630 hrs 16 May 1890 the *Dacca* struck Daedalus Shoal and sank later that day. There were no casualties amongst the 464 passenger and 91 crew. The official Enquiry blamed the loss on the unskilful navigation of First Officer James Tait and suspended his certificate for a period of 12 months (see also Rosario).

DAI HONG DAN – North Korean freighter damaged by mine in the Southern Red Sea on 2 August 1984. The vessel continued with its journey – no reported casualties.

DANA CORONA & DANA SIRENA – Former names of the *Al-Qamar Al-Saudi Al-Misri*.

DAREN VITIS – Little is known of this vessel which is supposed to have been lost somewhere off Hurghada. It is likely the name of this ship has been confused with the *Karin Vatis*.

DESPINA – Greek freighter of 3,016 grt built in 1907. On a voyage from Calcutta to Port Said with a cargo of coal, the *Despina* caught fire and was abandoned in the Red Sea. The vessel drifted towards Saudi Arabia and eventually sank of Râbigh on 19 July 1952.

DORA OLDENDORFF – Original name of the *Chrisoula K*.

DUPETIT THOARS – French destroyer which rescued the crew of Cypriot freighter *Trader* on 7 November 1987.

EDENMOOR – British freighter built by J. Readhead & Sons and completed in 1894. Her dimensions were 98m x 12.7m with a draught of 6.7m and a displacement of 3,107 grt. On 26 November 1897, the *Edenmoor* caught fire and sank of Jebeltier. Her cargo was mainly petroleum.

EGYPTIAN PATROL BOAT – Discovered by Lawson Wood at a depth of 38m southeast of Umm Qamar Island at GPS position 27° 20·100N, 33° 54·850E, this 25m Patrol Boat ran aground in the summer of 1962 and was lost. The vessel is now reduced to a tangle of pipes and debris.

EL GAMIL – Egyptian steamship built by Sunderland Shipbuilding Co and completed in 1904. Her dimensions were 75.9m x 11.1m with a draught of 6.5m and a displacement of 1,356 grt. On 25 October 1960, the *El Gamil* sank during a journey from Suez to Aden approx. 30 miles (48 km) NNW. of Abu Ail. 22 lives were lost.

ELLIOT – Panamanian registered general cargo vessel of 2,870 grt built in Bilbao and launched in 1963. On 11 July 1984, during a voyage from Syria to Bombay with a cargo of Chickpeas, the *Elliot* ran hard aground at position 28° 02' 06"N, 33° 23' 50"E and was abandoned as a constructive total loss.

ELVIRA – Panamanian registered steamship 1,584 grt. On 28 July 1968 during a voyage from Jeddah to Berbera the *Elvira* ran aground off Zuqar Island. The ship was later refloated and towed to Aden where she was declared a constructive total loss.

EMIL – Greek general cargo vessel built in Amsterdam and launched in 1958. Her dimensions were 119.49m x 15.02m with a draught of 8.08m and a displacement of 3,810 grt. On 10 December 1979, the fully loaded *Emil* was berthed in Port Sudan harbour when fire broke out following an explosion in her engine room. She was towed out of harbour and abandoned at position 19° 37' 30"N, 37° 17' 00"E.

ENY – Panamanian freighter of 1,053 grt. On 7 March 1969, during a journey from Jeddah to Suez in Ballast, the *Eny* was wrecked when she ran aground on Na'man Island.

ERMIONI – Former name of the *Safir*.

ESTE – Panamanian freighter damaged by mine in Gulf of Suez on 27 July 1984. The vessel continued with its journey – no reported casualties.

ETHA RICKMERS – Former name of the *Gladys Moller*.

EUROCARRIER – See *Nahed*.

EUROPA – Original name of the *Blue Sea*.

FARAH II – Panamanian roro motor ferry of 1,722 grt. On 6 March 1986 the *Farah II* was loading cars and passengers at the Egyptian port of Nuweiba in the Gulf of Aqaba when a fire broke out in the crew's accommodation. All persons on board safely disembarked before the listing ship was towed clear of the harbour. The large amounts of water used to extinguish the fire then caused the ship to capsize in 120m of water at GPS position 28° 56.6N, 34° 39·2E.

FENGSHUN – Former name of the *Million Hope*.

FILOTHEI – Greek freighter of 9,789 grt. On 23 May 1985 during a voyage from La Spezia to Karachi with a general cargo of 12,655 tonnes, the *Filothei* ran aground on Saba Island in the southern Red Sea. The ship was later declared a constructive total loss and was towed to Pakistan where she was broken up.

FIN – Small Newfoundland trader wrecked in the Red Sea on 13 February 1907.

FOTINI II – Cypriot freighter of 1,501 grt. On 14 July 1978, during a voyage from Assab to Jeddah with a cargo of coffee, the *Fotini II* suffered steering gear failure and ran aground in the Red Sea. On 15 July she refloated under her own power and proceeded to Jeddah where her cargo was unloaded. The ship was then declared a constructive total loss. On 26 March 1979, whilst unmanned at Jeddah Roads, the vessel then drifted aground on North Gateway reef during heavy weather and was wrecked.

FRANGESTAN – Hong Kong registered steel screw steamer of 8,228 grt built by Palmers of Newbridge and launched in January 1899. On 2 April 1924 the *Frangestan* was lost somewhere in the Red Sea.

FRED SCAMARONI – Original name of the *Salem Express*.

GENOVA – Former name of the *Urania*.

GEORG SCHUMANN – East German freighter damaged by mine in the southern Red Sea on 2 August 1984. The vessel continued with its journey – no reported casualties.

GISMATALLAH – Saudi Arabian freighter of 1,598 grt built in 1938. On an undeclared voyage, the *Gismatallah* was lost on Qwasiyah Reef, Jeddah Roads on 26 March 1979.

GLADYS MOLLER – British general cargo vessel built by A. Stephen & Sons Ltd of Glasgow and launched in 1906. Her dimensions were 122m x 15.85m with a draught of 7.55m and a displacement of 5,285 grt. Purchased by Moller Line in 1938, on 1 April 1942, she began the task of towing the damaged *Turbo* from Suez to Aden. Three days later, the *Turbo* broke in two during bad weather and was lost. On 7 November 1942, the *Gladys Moller* stranded on the east coast of Ceylon (now Sri Lanka) and was abandoned as a constructive total loss.

GLENTARA – Former name of the *Salamaua*

GULF FLEET NO 31 – Offshore support vessel built in 1978. Registered in New Orleans as part of the Gulf Fleet. After striking a Reef in 1985 the vessel was lost. In 2001 the wreck was discovered at a depth of 97m. Thought to be the wreck off the western coast of Umm Qamar Island at position 27° 20' 24"N, 33° 53' 57"E.

HALF WRECK AT FURY SHOAL – See *Adamantia K*.

HAMATA Name taken from the mountains near Marsa Sataya and given to the shipwrecks *Adamantia K*, *Hadia* and *Hamada* over time.

HARMEN OLDENDORFF – Original name of the *Olden*.

HAWK – According to the Red Sea Pilot published by Imray Laurie & Wilson, the wreck of the sailing yacht *Hawk* lies at 30m on the drop-off somewhere along the south of Zabargad Island. There are no further details.

HAZIM – Small cargo boat of 251 grt. On 19 August 1949, during a voyage from Alexandria to Jeddah with a cargo of tyres, tobacco and tea, the *Hazim* was lost at position 28° 18'N, 36° 12'E.

HELME PARK – Original name of the *Zealot*.

HENRY DEARBORN – US freighter which collided with the Cape Clear near Suez on 21 August 1944. The *Henry Dearborn* survived the collision and was repaired.

HEY DAROMA – See chapter on *Million Hope*.

HONG KONG – British Peninsular and Oriental Steam Navigation Company vessel of 3,174 grt built in Greenock and launched in May 1889. Wrongly described as being in the Egyptian Red Sea, the *Hong Kong* struck Azalea Reef, Yemen on 5 December 1890 and was lost.

HOPE – Immediate previous name of the *Million Hope*. The name changed only a few weeks before the vessel's final journey and *Hope* is the name under which the details of this ship are found in Lloyd's Register of Shipping.

HUI YANG – Chinese freighter damaged by mine in the Southern Red Sea on 31 July 1984. The vessel continued with its journey – no reported casualties.

HUNGARIA – Original name of the *Urania*.

IKE – American freighter of 7,209 grt built in 1945. On 29 November 1962, during a voyage to Saigon with an unspecified cargo she was lost on the Hanish Islands.

INDIAN ENTERPRISE – British cargo ship built by the Shipbuilding Corpn. (Wear Branch) and completed in 1946. Her dimensions were 131.4m x 17.2m with a draught of 10.8m and a displacement of 7,319 grt. The *Indian Enterprise* was on a journey from Bremen and London to Calcutta with a cargo which included 538 tons of explosives. On 19 June 1950, at position 25° 31' N, 35° 27' E in the Red Sea, this ship was destroyed by explosion. Only one survivor from a crew of 73.

IONA – Details of this vessel are not known. Apparently this ship hit a reef and sank off Yenbo, Saudi Arabia circa 1920.

IOULLIA – Greek merchant ship of 1,808 grt built in Frederickstad and launched in 1929. On 6 April 1969 with a cargo 3,200 tons of cement, the *Ioullia* caught fire and sank 75 miles south of Suez at position 28° 32' 42"N, 33° 02' 35"E. The vessel was abandoned without loss of life.

IRENE – Lebanese registered merchant ship of 1,499 grt built in 1913. On 29 November 1961, whilst in ballast from Mocha to Port Sudan she was lost on the reef outside Port Sudan harbour.

ISOLA DI LEVANZO – Original name of the *Levanzo*.

JASMINE – Unconfirmed name given to a small vessel thought to be from the early 1900's lost north of Sha'ab Ali at position 27° 54' 41"N, 33° 49' 26"E.

JERSEY – British freighter of 4,986 grt. On 23 April 1942 the *Jersey* struck a mine laid by U561 when coming in to anchor 1.45 nautical miles southwest of Western Beacon in Suez Bay. Possibly the wreck marked on Chart 2375 at position 29° 50' 30"N, 32° 32' 30"E.

JOLANDE- Incorrect spelling of *JOLANDA*.

JORK – Panamanian cargo vessel of 908 grt built by J. J. Sietas of Hamburg and launched in 1971. On 27 May 1986, during a journey from Bombay to Suez with a cargo of 2,000 tons of bagged Soya beans, the *Jork* sank in the northern Red Sea after striking bottom.

JOZEF WYBICKI – Polish freighter of 8,644 grt built in 1967. On 11 August 1984, during a journey from the Far East to Gdynia with a general cargo, the *Jozef Wybicki* struck a mine in the southern Red Sea. The ship continued to Suez at half speed and eventually arrived at her home port of Gdynia in September. Subsequent survey revealed she had sustained damage so severe she was declared a constructive total loss and sold for scrap.

KAPITAN KISSA – Ukrainian bulk carrier of 6,210 grt built in Leningrad and launched in 1974. On 13 July 1996, during a journey to Jeddah in ballast the *Kapitan Kissa* ran aground in the Straits of Tiran and was re-floated 2 days later.

KARIN VATIS – Greek bulk carrier of 22,114 grt. On 16 November 1985 with a cargo of 31,620 tons of scrap metal the *Karin Vatis* developed a leak and eventually sank at position 25° 13'N, 35° 44'E – in over 600m of water.

KASTORIA – Former name of the *Adamantia K*.

HMS KHARTOUM – British Destroyer of 1,690 grt built by Swan Hunter and launched on 6 February 1939. On 23 June 1940, while operating in the southern Red Sea, HMS *Khartoum* was wrecked by an internal explosion. The captain managed to beach the ship on Perim Island, South Yemen where she was abandoned.

KIMON – Former name of the *Kimon M*.

KNUD JESPERSON – Russian roro/general cargo vessel damaged by mine in the Gulf of Suez on 9 July 1984. The vessel continued with its journey – no reported casualties.

KOHOLYT – Former name of the *Adamantia K*.

KORMORAN – Original name of the *Zingara*.

KOMSOMOLETS BYELORUSSII – Original name of the *Kapitan Kissa*.

KOSTI – Former name of the *Tirrenia*.

KRITI CORAL – Greek freighter damaged by mine off Hodeidah in the Southern Red Sea on 2 August 1984. The vessel continued with its journey – no reported casualties.

KROHN TRADER – Former name of the *Lara*.

LABANZO – Incorrect name given to the *Levanzo*.

LAEICZ – German steel screw steamer of 4,500 grt built in Flensburg and launched in 1901. On 16 March 1908 the *Laeicz* was lost somewhere in the Red Sea.

LAIRDS LOCH – Original name of the *Hey Daroma* (see chapter on *Million Hope*).

LATIF – Screw corvette and, in 1877, third most important warship in the Egyptian Navy. In March 1877, the *Latif* transported Colonel Gordon RE (Gordon Pasha) to the Sudan.

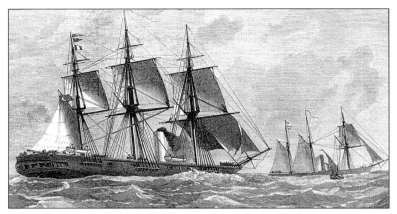

The *Latif* en route for the Sudan carrying Colonel Gordon RE (Gordon Pasha).

(Illustrated London News Picture Library)

In April 1877, the ship was returning to Egypt carrying Egyptian troops home from Abyssinia plus approx. 100 passengers and crew when the vessel caught fire some miles from the coast. Panic quickly spread amongst the troops even though two ships were on hand and bravely came alongside to rescue all on board. The *Latif's* own guns where fully loaded and the flames caused them to fire indiscriminately. The lack of discipline amongst the troops was later cited as the sole reason for the deaths of 30 people.

LEVANZO – Italian steel screw steamer of 3,875 grt built in Leghorn and launched in 1901. On 14 March 1923 the *Levanzo* drove hard onto Elba Reef in north Sudanese waters and was lost. This wreck is approx. 21 hours sailing time from Port Sudan.

LINERA – Cypriot freighter damaged by mine in the Gulf of Suez on 28 July 1984. The vessel continued with its journey – no reported casualties.

LINNGSBON – Former name of the *Million Hope*.

LORD SINAI – Former name of the *Salem Express*.

LORI R – Former name of the *Safir*.

LOUILLA – Incorrect name given to *Loullia*.

LOULLIA – Panamanian freighter of 2,271 grt built in Sweden and launched in May 1952. On 29 September 1981, during a voyage from Aqaba to Suez in ballast, the *Loullia* ran hard onto Gordon Reef in the Straits of Tiran. The crew safely abandoned ship and her remains are still found on top of the reef at position 27° 59' 30"N, 34° 27' 12"E.

MAGNA – Original name of the *Ioullia*.

MALDIVE TRANSPORT – British freighter of 4,907 grt built in Hartlepool and launched in 1952. On 29 April 1972, during a voyage from Bangkok to Safaga and Aqaba, fire broke out in No. 3 Hold when in the Egyptian Red Sea. The fire spread to the engine room and the ship was beached approx. 3 miles south of Safaga. The *Maldive Transport* then drifted south for another 2 miles before becoming stranded. The ship was completely gutted by the fire and abandoned as a constructive total loss.

MARATHON – Former name of the *Tirrenia*.

MARCUS – See *Markos*.

MARIA SCHRÖDER – German freighter of 1,906 grt built in Trondheim and launched in 1920. On 11 April 1956, during a voyage from Aqaba to Suez in ballast, The *Maria Schröder* encountered heavy weather and ran aground approx. 25 miles north of Sharm el Sheikh. Still found on top of the Reef at position 28° 11' 30"N, 34° 28' 00"E.

MARIENBURG – Original name of the *Adamantia K*.

MARINER II – Panamanian bulk carrier of 10,099 grt built in Osaka and launched in 1968. On 23 April 1985, during a voyage from Yugoslavia to Bangkok and Hong Kong with a cargo of 14,800 tons of iron products, the *Mariner II* sank in deep water off Safaga after striking a mine. All 29 crew were safely rescued.

MARKO – See *Markos*.

MARKOS – Former name of *Giannis D*. Sometimes also wrongly called *Marko*, *Markos D*, *Markus* and even *Marcus*.

MARKO TASILO – Yugoslav general cargo vessel of 1,851 grt built at Fredrikstad and launched in 1951. On 12 July 1990, during a voyage from Aden to Suez in ballast, the *Marko Tasilo* sank after a collision with the *Atlantic Trader 1* off Jabal Attair Island. All crew members were safely rescued by the *Atlantic Trader 1* which proceeded to Aden for repairs.

MARKUS – See *Markos*.

MARSEILLAIS 9 – Small French vessel of 149 grt lost on Sha'ab Ali on 29 March 1928. Although the name appears to be spelt incorrectly, this is the spelling used in the Lloyd's Wreck Returns for 1928.

MATAURA – Original name of the *Hadia*.

MEDI SEA – Liberian freighter damaged by mine in the Gulf of Suez on 27 July 1984. The vessel continued with its journey – no reported casualties.

MED SEA – Former name of the *AL KAHFAIN*.

MEIYO MARU – Japanese vehicle transporter damaged by mine in the Gulf of Suez on 27 July 1984. The vessel continued with its journey – no reported casualties.

MILVERTON – Original name of *Salamaua*.

MORGUL – Turkish freighter damaged by mine in the Southern Red Sea on 2 August 1984. The vessel continued with its journey – no reported casualties.

MUSHTERI – Small Turkish cargo boat of 636 grt. On 30 May 1909, during a voyage to Hodeidah with a general cargo, the *Mushteri* was lost on Boheira Reef, Jeddah.

The *Latif* on fire. (Illustrated London News Picture Library)

MUSTAPHA BEY – Former name of the *Turc*.

HMS *Myngs* – Original name of the *El Qaher*.

NAHED – Saudi Arabian livestock carrier of 3,152 grt built by Ansaldo of Genoa and launched in 1948. On 30 October 1977, whilst outward bound from Jeddah, the *Nahed* sank after colliding with the inbound *Eurocarrier*. Three crew were killed. The *Nahed* was later cut up and dumped in deep water. The *Eurocarrier* was able to continue its journey.

NAZARIO SAURO – Italian cargo/passenger ship of 8,150 grt also built by Ansaldo of Genoa and launched in May 1921. Intended as a cargo ship, she was redesigned during construction to accommodate passengers in response to the growing number of emigrants to America. She later saw service as a troopship. In 1940 Italy entered the War and the *Nazario Sauro* was caught in the Red Sea where she was laid up in Massawa until April 1941. With Eritrea about to fall into British hands, the ship was moved to the Dahlak Islands and scuttled.

The *Nazario Sauro*. (World Ship Society)

NEERA – British cargo ship built by A. Leslie & Co and completed in 1868. Her dimensions were 100.7m x 10.5m with a draught of 7.6m and a displacement of 2,167 grt. On 21 February 1884, the *Neera* was wrecked on Sha'ab Mobryeet Reef, in the Red Sea.

NEPTUNA – German-owned dive boat which sank off Zabargad Island during the eighties.

NICOLAOS A MASTRANDREAS – Greek freighter of 2,387 grt sank at Port Ibrahim, near Suez on 5 December 1967 after a fire broke out in her engine room.

NIMOS – Greek general cargo vessel built in Italy and launched in 1950. Her dimensions were 97.21m x 14.08m with a draught of 8.92m and a displacement of 2,093 grt. On 21 March 1978, during a journey from Jeddah to Port Sudan, the *Nimos* ran aground at position 19° 29'N, 37° 24'E. She was carrying a general cargo plus 123 cars. After stranding, the weather deteriorated and lifeboats were smashed against the hull. The crew then took to the life-rafts from which all 18 were safely rescued. The *Nimos* was later abandoned as a constructive total loss.

NINA – Original name of the *Agia Varvara*.

NOPAL TRADER – Original name of the *Lara*.

NUITS SAINT GEORGE – Former name of the *Salem Express*.

OLAV RINGDAL JR – See *Tirrenia*.

OLDEN – Panamanian registered bulk carrier of 27,288 grt. See chapter 10.

OLIGARCH – Royal Fleet Auxiliary ship of 6,897 grt built by Workman, Clark and Co. of Belfast and launched in 1918. Her dimensions were 135.4m x 17.42m with a draught of 8.3m (fully loaded). On 14 April 1946, with a cargo of poisonous gas shells, the Oligarch was scuttled in the northern Red Sea at position 27° 30'N, 34° 45'E in over 900m of water.

ORPHEUS – Greek bulk carrier of 15,553 grt built in 1961. On 17 June 1979, during a voyage from Piraeus to Yenbo, Saudi Arabia with a cargo of bulk cement, the *Orpheus* struck Shuaiba Reef, Saudi Arabia in position 24° 25' 48"N, 37° 08' 00"E and was lost. The 29 man crew were all safely rescued.

ORREHOLM – Former name of the *Hadia*.

PACIFIC ROYAL – Former name of the *Million Hope*.

PALAMCOTTA – Vessel belonging to British India Associated Steamers which, along with the *Rosario*, rescued 464 passenger and 91 crew from the stricken *Dacca* which struck Daedalus Shoal and sank on 16 May 1890. On arrival at Suez, the *Palamcotta* was then made ready to take some of the passengers to Australia.

PARAMATTA – Small British sailing cargo ship of 400 grt built in Sunderland in the 1840's and lost somewhere in the Red Sea whilst on a voyage to London.

PAT 4 – Kuwaiti freighter of 1,923 grt built in 1951. On 28 June 1979, during a voyage from Hamriyah to Suez with a general cargo, the *Pat 4* struck Hamriyah Breakwater in heavy weather and sank.

PERA ALMA or PERRA ALMA – Occasionally wrongly reported as being in the Egyptian Red Sea, this is one of two wrecks reported off the Hanish Islands – which lie midway between Eritrea and Yemen. The islands belong to Eritrea and little is known about this wreck. Either spelling of this name may be slightly incorrect.

Peruvian Reefer – Bahamian freighter damaged by mine in the Southern Red Sea on 31 July 1984. The vessel continued with its journey – no reported casualties.

PETROS – Former name of the *Agia Varvara*.

PINE – Former name of the *Shiqma*.

PLASTIC WRECK – See *Hadia*.

POLIAGOS – Cypriot freighter of 3,371 grt built in Holland and launched in 1947. With a cargo of 5,000 tons of cement, the *Poliagos* struck Shadwan Island on 28 December 1980 while avoiding another vessel. This is thought to be the wreck on the north side of Shadwan Island in an out-of-bounds area at position 27° 30' 30"N, 34° 00' 23"E.

POSEIDONIA – Former name of the *AL KAHFAIN*.

PURFINA CONGO – Motor tanker which struck the P & O passenger-cargo ship Shillong amidships on 22 October 1957 resulting in the loss of the *Shillong*.

ROLF JARL – Former name of the *Maria Schröder*.

RONALDSHAY – Indian dredger of 1,023 grt built by W. Simons & Co. and launched in 1922. On 21 October 1942 the *Ronaldshay* was torpedoed and sunk by German aircraft immediately outside the Egyptian Military base at Safaga. The Captain and approx. 52 crew were lost in the attack. In the 1960's the wreck attracted its first scuba divers and was immediately placed out-of-bounds by the Egyptian authorities. In 1987, demolition of this 78m wreck commenced and took 3 years to complete.

ROSARIO – (I am indebted to Radhika Kumar – a distant descendant of Captain William Brown of Hull (1855-1893) who recently inherited papers belonging to the late master mariner which includes a copy of the undermentioned testimonial). The *Rosario* was a vessel belonging to British India Associated Steamers which, under command of Captain Brown, was the first ship to render assistance to the Dacca which struck Daedalus Shoal on 16 May 1890 and sank. Along with the *Palamcotta*, these two ships rescued 464 passenger and 91 crew and almost all the cabin baggage. For his heroic efforts, Captain Brown received a written testimonial signed by 14 of the rescued 'Saloon' passengers plus the *Dacca's* Surgeon Superintendent. Captain Brown also later received a gold watch from the *Dacca's* owners.

RYGJA – Original name of the *Tirrenia*.

RYUSEI MARU – Original name of the *Million Hope*.

SACH – Former name of the *Safir*.

SADAKA – Saudi Arabian freighter of 1,112 grt built in Turku, Finland and launched in 1963. On 5 September 1980, the *Sadaka* experienced engine failure and ran aground on Mismari Reef where she was wrecked. Her final position is recorded as 20° 19' 30"N, 39° 05' 54"E. The cargo of 3,000 live sheep perished.

SAD EL FURAT – Egyptian motor-tanker of 13,235 grt built in Hamburg and launched in 1960. During hostilities on 4 April 1969, the *Sad el Furat* caught fire whilst alongside a terminal jetty at Suez. The ship eventually sank about one week later.

SAFIR – Panamanian freighter of 8,932 grt built by Austin & Pickersgill of Sunderland and launched in January 1973. On 12 September 1989, with a cargo of 14,700 tons of rock phosphate from Aqaba, the *Safir* struck a reef near Tiran Island at position 27° 59' 12"N, 34° 26' 12"E. Salvage operations commenced and the ship was refloated. On 18 September, whilst under tow, however, the *Safir* finally sunk at position 27° 47' 00"N, 34° 24' 18"E in over 1000m of water. There were no casualties

SALAMAUA – British freighter of 6,676 grt built by Harland & Wolff and launched in 1920. During the same period in which the Thistlegorm and Rosalie Moller were lost, the *Salamaua* was also bombed and badly damaged in the Gulf of Suez. This ship, however, was repaired and went on to survive the war.

SAMAH – Egyptian roro cargo vessel of 597 grt built in the Teraoka shipyard in Nandan and launched in 1976. On 12 November 1992, during a voyage from Suez to Jeddah, the *Samah* sank in position 28° 18' 16"N, 33° 09' 14"E. All crew were safely rescued.

SAMARAH – Former name of the Hamada.

SAO THOMÉ – Portuguese iron screw steamer of 2,255 grt built by Earle's of Hull and launched in June 1883. On 25 November 1904 this very elegant ship was lost in the Gulf of Suez.

SARAH H – See chapter on the *Kingston*.

SCALARIA – British medium tanker built by Swan Hunter & Wigham Richardson and launched in 1922. Her dimensions were 125.3m x 16.2m with a draught of 9.4m and a displacement of 5,683 grt. On 19 October 1942, the *Scalaria* was attacked by enemy aircraft off Râs Gharib in the Gulf of Suez and sank at position 28° 20' 42"N, 33° 07' 12"E with the loss of 11 lives. The Captain survived. This wreck is found in an out-of-bounds area of the Gulf of Suez and in 2002 was described by the UK Hydrographic Office as "Dangerous."

SCOL VALIANT – Former name of the *Jork*.

SCHILDTURM – Small supply vessel of 497 grt built in 1968. On 14 February 1979, whilst operating near an offshore oil-field, this vessel was beached near Râs Gharib after striking a wreck. She was subsequently abandoned as a constructive total loss.

SEASTAR – In addition to this name being wrongly given to the *Kimon M* and *Chrisoula K*, there are also unsubstantiated rumours of another wreck supposedly bearing this name somewhere off Gobal Sheghir. No evidence of any vessel bearing this name and having been lost in the Red Sea is yet forthcoming.

SEVERN – Former name of the *Turc*.

SHEIKH BERKHUD – Small Egyptian cargo boat of 473 grt. On 31 October 1926, during a voyage from Suez to Port Sudan with a general cargo, the *Sheikh Berkhud* was lost somewhere in the Red Sea.

SHILLONG – British P & O passenger-cargo ship of 8,934 grt built by Vickers Armstrong and launched in March 1949. On 22 October 1957, during a journey from Hamburg to Tsingtao with a general cargo of 11,700 tons and 6 passengers, the *Shillong* was struck amidships on the port side by the motor tanker *Purfina Congo* and later sank in position 28° 16' 33"N, 33° 13' 50"E. Two members of crew were lost and a third died later from injuries sustained when boarding a lifeboat.

SHIMQA – Incorrect spelling of *Shiqma*

The *Scalaria*. Note how very similar this ship is to the *Turbo* (Chapter 17) which was built 10 years earlier. (Shell Photographic Services)

The *Shillong* at Hong Kong in 1949. (P&O Archives/QFT Photography)

SHIQMA – Israeli container ship of 6,277 grt. On 25 May 1981, during a journey from Eilat to South Africa with containerised cargo, the *Shiqma* developed a serious list and then sank at position 18° 28'N, 39° 23'E – approximately 150 miles southeast of Port Sudan in over 700m of water. Although launched as the *Shiqma* in 1965, she was renamed *Pine* in 1974 but reverted to her original name the following year.

SHOYO MARU – Original name of the *Giannis D.*

SIRIS – (I am indebted to Captain Dany Nakdimon – former master of the *Siris* – for explaining how his ship was refloated and towed away for scrap in 1978 and for very kindly providing two photographs confirming this.). Liberian tanker of 29,592 grt built in Japan and launched in 1960. On 26 October 1973, during a journey from Eilat to Abu Rudeis in ballast, the *Siris* struck a mine in the Gulf of Suez and eventually sank off the Ashrafi Islands. Originally thought to be the wreck marked on Admiralty Chart 2375 at 27° 47' 37"N, 33° 42' 09"E, we enjoyed a long and fruitless search for this wreck before hearing from Captain Nakdimon.

The *Siris* after having been raised and about to be towed away for scrapping. (Captain Dany Nakdimon)

The *Siris* shortly after having been sunk by a mine in the Gulf of Suez. (Captain Dany Nakdimon)

SMIT-LLOYD 10 – Dutch motor-tug/supply vessel of 784 grt owned and operated by Smit-Lloyd BV. On 30 September 1978, the *Smit-Lloyd 10* struck an oil rig in the Morgan Oilfield and sank at position 28° 12' 12"N, 33° 26' 19"E. Her seven man crew were all safely rescued.

SOELA – Former name of the *Ioullia*.

STAR OF RAWIAH – Saudi Arabian freighter of 778 grt built in 1943. On 6 April 1972, during a voyage from Suez to Safaga in ballast she ran aground and was abandoned as a constructive total loss. This small vessel is thought to be the wreck marked on Admiralty Chart 2375 at position 27° 48' 00"N, 33° 40' 16"E. In July 2002 we conducted a search for this wreck but were unable to discover any remains whatsoever.

STEEL SEAFARER – American freighter of 5,719 grt built in 1921. On 6 September 1941, the *Steel Seafarer* was bombed and sunk by German Aircraft in the vicinity of Shadwan Island. Last reported position was 27° 20'N, 34° 15'E. There were no casualties.

SUMATRA – Peninsular and Oriental Steam Navigation Company passenger steamer built by Derry & Co. of Dumbarton and launched on 13 September 1867. Her dimensions were 97.03m x 11.68m with a draught of 8.03m and a displacement of 2,488 grt. In addition to sails fore and aft, she was also equipped with a single steam piston engine capable of providing a top speed of 13 knots. In 1869, the *Sumatra* rescued the survivors of the *Carnatic* and delivered them safely to Suez. In May 1886, however, she was sold to Hajee Cassum Joosub of Bombay and used for the Mecca pilgrimage trade. On 4 March 1889, the *Sumatra* caught fire and was lost in the Southern Red Sea. Her final position is not known.

TAIWAN – Twin screw freighter owned by Wilhelm Wilhermsen of Tönsberg, Norway, built by Deutsche Werft A. G. of Hamburg and launched in July 1924. On 14 March 1950, the *Taiwan* ran aground on Rocky Island and, although later refloated, was eventually abandoned at sea – afloat but in a sinking condition. The *Taiwan* was never seen again and finally sank somewhere in the southern Egyptian Red Sea.

The *Taiwan.* (World Ship Society)

TALITA – Maltese general cargo vessel of 1,365 grt built in Holland and launched in 1967. On 15 June 1988, during a voyage from Greece to Port Sudan, the *Talita* ran aground near Râs Gharib. The crew safely abandoned the stricken vessel which later sank at position 28° 38' 14"N, 32° 59' 00"E.

The *Talita*. (World Ship Society)

TAMARA II – Panamanian freighter of 8,420 grt built in Uddevalla and launched in 1960. On 10 March 1983, with a cargo of 12,000 tons of bagged cement, the *Tamara II* ran aground on Sha'ab Ashrafi. This is the wreck marked on Admiralty Chart 2375 at position 27° 49' 12"N, 33° 38' 24"E. The entire vessel sits almost high and dry on top of the reef and from a distance still looks as though she is intact.

TAMIM I – Egyptian motor tanker of 791 grt built in Holland and launched in 1953. On 3 October 1983, during a journey from Suez to Bernese with a cargo of 900 tons of bitumen oil, the *Tamim I* caught fire and was abandoned by her crew. Thought to be the wreck shown on Admiralty Chart 2375 at position 27° 46' 00"N, 33° 36' 58"E.

TANG HE – Chinese container vessel damaged by a mine in the southern Red Sea on 3 August 1984. The vessel continued with its journey – no reported casualties.

TAROBA – See *Dacca* and *Rosario*.

TASEER – United Arab Emirates general cargo vessel built in Sweden and launched in 1952. Her dimensions were 94.14m x 13.75m with a draught of 6.0m and a displacement of 1,900 grt. Whilst laid up at Jeddah, the *Taseer* was sold to Pakistani ship-breakers and duly sailed for Gadani Beach. On 4 April 1986 she ran aground at Sha'ab Loka in position 18° 44'N, 38° 33'E. Salvage tugs were unable to refloat the ship which was later abandoned as a constructive total loss.

TATIANGELA – Greek freighter of 419 grt built in 1955. On 4 January 1979, during a voyage from Assab to Jeddah with a cargo of coffee, horse beans and pumpkin seeds, the *Tatiangela* suffered main engine damage during heavy weather. She eventually sank in position 19° 18'N, 39° 53'E approximately 160 miles east of Port Sudan in over 300m of water.

TETI NOMICOS – Former name of the *Adamantia K*.

THEOUPOLIS – Cypriot freighter damaged by a mine in the southern Red Sea on 15 August 1984. The vessel continued with its journey – no reported casualties.

TIENSIN and TIENSTIN – Incorrect names given to the British Admiralty tugboat *Tien Hsing* (see Part One of this Appendix).

TILE WRECK – Local name given to the *Chrisoula K* on account of her cargo.

TIMALEXANDRIA – Egyptian motor supply vessel of 697 grt built at Wallsend-on-Tyne and launched in 1965. On 5 September 1984, the *Timalexandria* struck unmarked underwater tanks when coming alongside the quay at Râs Gharib. All attempts to refloat the ship were unsuccessful and she was later abandoned as a constructive total loss.

TIRRENIA – Finnish freighter of 3,957 grt built in Sunderland and launched in 1905. During a journey from Costanza to China with a cargo of ammonium nitrate, the *Tirrenia* caught fire east of Port Sudan. At 2258 hrs (GMT) 23 January 1953, the master of passing motor tanker Olav Ringdal Jr reported the *Tirrenia* exploded and sank at position 19° 11'N, 39° 18'E and that the crew were now safe on board his ship.

TRADER – Cypriot freighter of 9,305 grt built in 1969. On 7 November 1987, during a journey from Augusta to China, this ship sank at position 24° 23'N, 36° 12'E after her engine room became flooded. The crew of 23 were all safely rescued by the French destroyer *Dupetit Thoars*.

TRAWLER – Unnamed Russian trawler damaged by a mine off the Hanish islands on 14 August 1984. The vessel continued with its journey – no reported casualties.

TREKRONER – Original name of *Al-Qamar Al-Saudi Al-Misri*.

Tug/Supply vessel (Unknown). During a dedicated wreck search in 2002, we came across this wreck which is marked on Admiralty Chart 2375 at position 27° 51' 42"N, 33° 48' 49"E. She lies up on top of the reef and appears to be an unknown tug/supply vessel of a type commonly used by the local oil industry.

TURC – Turkish iron screw steamer of 1,736 grt built in Sunderland and launched in April 1873. Later renamed *Severn*. In May 1895, the *Turc* ran aground and broke in two on Abu Madafi Reef approximately 40 miles north of Jeddah at position 22° 03'N, 38° 45'E and became a constructive total loss. No lives were lost.

ULSTER QUEEN – Former name of the *Al Kahfain*.

UMBRIA – Italian twin-screw passenger cargo vessel of 10,076 grt built by Rieherst Schiffswerks of Hamburg and launched in December 1911. On 10 June 1940, with a cargo of 360,000 bombs, 60 boxes of detonators and other stores, the *Umbria* was scuttled close inshore near Port Sudan by her Captain – whilst a Royal Navy boarding party were actually on board and searching the ship for contraband! After the War, a British bomb-disposal expert reported that, in the event of an explosion, half of Port Sudan was likely to disappear. Vessel and cargo are all still there in shallow water…

URANIA – Italian twin-screw passenger-cargo vessel of 7,099 grt built by Cantiere San Rocco SA of Trieste and launched in September 1916. Like the *Nazario Sauro*, the *Urania* was trapped in the Red Sea when Italy finally entered WW2 in 1940 and was immediately laid up at Massawa. The ship was moved to the Dahlak Islands and scuttled on 10 April 1941.

VALENCIA – Spanish tanker damaged by a mine in the Gulf of Suez on 28 July 1984. The vessel continued with its journey – no reported casualties.

VIKI K – Greek general cargo vessel of 5,936 grt built in Lübeck and launched in 1952. On 2 November 1981, during a voyage from Bilbao to Bandar Khomeini, the *Viki K* was abandoned in a sinking condition in the Gulf of Suez at position 27° 38' 00"N, 33° 42' 00"E. This ship was supposed to be carrying a 10,000 tonne cargo valued at over £4M and

The *Umbria* circa 1937. (Lloyd Triestino di Navigazione SpA)

was later presumed to have sunk. Subsequent investigations, however, revealed her cargo was offloaded at Port Said. The *Viki K* was one of a number of vessels owned by a Mr Kavadas – one of which was reported as having sunk twice! Mr Kavadas disappeared before facing trial. Worth a serious search (for the wreck that is!).

WARWICKSHIRE – See chapter on *Maidan*.

HMS *WESSEX* – Original name of HMS *Zenith*.

WINE WRECK – Local name given to the *Carnatic* on account of the bottles found on board.

WINNER – Nothing is known of this vessel reported lost on the Brothers Islands.

WOOD WRECK – Local name given to the *Giannis D* on account of her cargo.

HMS *ZENITH* – Sister ship of HMS *Myngs* – see *El Qaher*.

ZINOVIA – Greek freighter of 8,393 grt. On 24 August 1979, during a voyage from Dunkirk to Port Sudan, with a cargo of 12,024 tonnes of bagged sugar, the *Zinovia* ran aground off Râs Gharib in the Gulf of Suez. After offloading a large amount of cargo, the ship was refloated and taken to Suez where she was declared a constructive total loss. In February 1980, the ship was towed to Port Sudan and the remainder of her cargo unloaded. The ship was then sold to Taiwanese breakers but, on 26 March 1980, during the voyage to Kaohsiung, the towline had to be cut because of bad weather and the *Zinovia* was driven aground on Duhrab Island. On 12 October 1980, she was refloated yet again, towed to Djibouti for temporary seaworthiness repairs after which she was towed to Gadani Beach in Pakistan and finally broken up.

ZSCHOPAU – Former name of the Loullia.

PART THREE

Missing Ships in the Gulf of Suez

The Gulf of Suez is an important international shipping link which ultimately joins the northern sectors of the Atlantic and Indian Oceans. The region also has another very important role for the Egyptian economy in terms of oil and gas production. Consequently, there are large areas which are placed out-of-bounds to all surface craft not actively engaged in those industries. Elsewhere, the relevant charts clearly show many places where all fishing and anchoring is strictly prohibited. The Gulf of Suez is also relatively shallow – being no more than 80m at its deepest. By comparison, the Gulf of Aqaba is up to 1800m deep.

A combination of the factor of; heavy surface traffic heading to and from the Suez Canal, oil and gas exploration (plus all the vessels, platforms, wells, derricks, pipelines, buoys etc), relatively shallow depth and somewhat confined area, has its consequences for scuba divers with much of the Gulf of Suez being out-of-bounds to diving boats. Furthermore, the underwater visibility is much reduced because of disturbed sediment. This tends to stifle coral growth and generally makes the area less attractive in any event. On the plus side, however, there does exist a good number of very exciting virgin shipwrecks which will instantly attract Scuba Divers in great numbers should the region ever be opened to diving. Whilst some could never be considered as serious diving prospects – either because they are high and dry up on top of the reef, too deep, located right in the middle of a very busy shipping channel or still found in an out-of-bounds area, there will still be plenty to whet the appetite. Altogether, those ships known to have been lost in the Gulf of Suez (in addition to those that are not known!) are a very exciting challenge indeed and perhaps one which we might all enjoy – one day!

From an imaginary line drawn between Bluff Point and Beacon Rock – as an entrance to the Gulf of Suez, I found 40 charted shipwrecks north of that line. Three of the marks relate to the *Kingston*, *Thistlegorm* and *Ulysses*. Another is the *Brick Wreck* mentioned in Part One of this Appendix and seventeen are mentioned in Part Two. From those forty positions, therefore, thirty-six are virtually unexplored of which nineteen are not even identified. One intriguing footnote, the *Dunraven* is not marked on any chart and one cannot help but wonder just how many more shipwrecks might be found in this testing stretch of water...

From North to South, the 40 marked positions are reproduced below. Where the name of a ship is included, I regard this as the most likely identity of the wreck in question – but most are not yet confirmed:

Striped Butterflyfish.

1. 29° 50' 30"N, 32° 32' 30"E. (*Jersey*)
2. 28° 38' 14"N, 32° 59' 00"E. (*Talita*)
3. 28° 32' 42"N, 33° 02' 35"E. (*Ioullia*)
4. 28° 31' 48"N, 33° 01' 24"E.
5. 28° 29' 36"N, 32° 59' 24"E.
6. 28° 28' 10"N, 33° 06' 12"E.
7. 28° 22' 00"N, 33° 12' 00"E. (*Cape Clear*)
8. 28° 20' 42"N, 33° 07' 12"E. (*Scalaria*)
9. 28° 19' 30"N, 33° 07' 00"E.
10. 28° 17' 00"N, 33° 08' 56"E.
11. 28° 16' 33"N, 33° 13' 50"E. (*Shillong*)
12. 28° 15' 00"N, 33° 16' 24"E.
13. 28° 14' 31"N, 33° 25' 37"E.
14. 28° 12' 49"N, 33° 37' 12"E.
15. 28° 12' 12"N, 33° 26' 19"E. (*Smit Lloyd 10*)
16. 28° 10' 42"N, 33° 20' 48"E.
17. 28° 09' 56"N, 33° 25' 59"E. (*Cristobal*)
18. 28° 09' 24"N, 33° 15' 48"E.
19. 28° 09' 24"N, 33° 16' 00"E.
20. 28° 08' 42"N, 33° 15' 36"E.
21. 28° 08' 24"N, 33° 21' 00"E.
22. 28° 02' 06"N, 33° 23' 50"E. (*Elliot*)
23. 27° 59' 58"N, 33° 28' 00"E.
24. 27° 59' 34"N, 33° 28' 36"E. (*Attiki*)
25. 27° 54' 48"N, 33° 53' 26"E.
26. 27° 54' 41"N, 33° 49' 26"E. (*Jasmine*)
27. 27° 51' 42"N, 33° 48' 49"E. (*Tug/Supply vessel*)
28. 27° 49' 49"N, 33° 43' 20"E.
29. 27° 49' 12"N, 33° 38' 24"E. (*Tamara II*)
30. 27° 49' 09"N, 33° 39' 18"E. (*Bacchis*)
31. 27° 48' 51"N, 33° 55' 13"E. (*Thistlegorm*)
32. 27° 48' 18"N, 33° 42' 40"E.
33. 27° 48' 03"N, 33° 44' 00"E.
34. 27° 48' 00"N, 33° 40' 16"E. (*Star of Rawiah*)
35. 27° 47' 46"N, 33° 51' 20"E. (*Brick Wreck*)
36. 27° 47' 37"N, 33° 42' 09"E.
37. 27° 46' 42"N, 33° 52' 36"E. (*Kingston*)
38. 27° 46' 00"N, 33° 36' 58"E. (*Tamim 1*)
39. 27° 44' 30"N, 33° 51' 56"E. (*Al-Qamar Al-Saudi Al-Misri*)
40. 27° 41' 12"N, 33° 48' 10"E. (*Ulysses*)

• ACKNOWLEDGEMENTS •

This book has taken over ten years to complete and would not have been possible without the support and assistance of a great many people. These include those who provided the inspiration, helped with personal diving equipment and photography, arranged my visits, excess baggage, the all-important diving, and those who assisted with the research. Along the way there were many individual contributions. In some cases these were nothing more than a ship's name, position or an address. At the other end of the scale, a safari boat was placed at my disposal for a whole week. Not least of these were a great many paying guests who tolerated me, my cameras and both my jokes during what was their own diving holiday. I only wish it was possible to mention each and every fellow diver by name. Big or small, each contribution was equally important and those named below are mentioned in no order of priority whatsoever. To each individual, organisation, institution and their staff plus the many divers I met along the way – I just want to say 'Thank you all, very much'.

I wish to pay special tribute to: Dr Bob Ballard for providing the inspiration for a book of this quality, to Rico Oldfield for enabling me to

Lionfish are found throughout the Red Sea.

realise the objective, to John Bantin for suggesting I contact Rico, to Ann Johnson for telling me to try Immel Publishing again and to David Elliott who was instrumental in bringing everything to fruition.

Personal Diving Equipment: I am frequently asked about my personal diving equipment. Most of what I do comes from my extensive experience of diving. I first learned to dive in 1976 and qualified as an Advanced Instructor & First Class Diver in 1980. I have remained an active diver throughout those years although I am not a technical diver. I am, however, a heavy user of air and for many years struggled to complete my work using the standard 12L cylinder. Larger cylinders were simply not available in Egypt and this made my work very difficult indeed. It was then that Gary Hamilton, of Slough Scuba Schools, gave me some much-needed advice and suggested I purchase twinning bands for my Buddy Commando BCD. From that moment on I used twinned 12L Cylinders coupled with a pair of Poseidon Cyklon Regulators and all previous difficulties disappeared. Then, in 2000, I was also introduced to the new Scubapro 'Twin Jet' fins. As much as I may try and keep myself fit I was, by this time, fifty-years-old and my days of winning the regimental mile were a very distant memory. These fins, however, had a revolutionary new design which proved to be a great energy saver. Finally, the repetitive diving required of me in the course of my work would not have been possible without my Aladin Air computer. Thank you Gary, AP Valves, Poseidon Diving Systems (Brian Bickell) and Scubapro UK Ltd (Nick Bailey, James Lutener, Andy Shears).

The Hawksbill Turtle is regularly encountered while
wreck diving in the Egyptian Red Sea.

Photographic Equipment: All my cameras and lenses are made by Nikon (supplied by Grays of Westminster). Aluminium housings are made by Aquatica of Canada (supplied by Backscatter Underwater Photo & Video, USA). TTL modifications were designed, made and fitted by David Knight (Cameras Underwater, UK). All strobes are by Ikelite. My favourite combination for wreck photography is – Nikon F3 camera, Nikkor 20mm wide-angle lens, Aquatica 3 housing, Ikelite Substrobe 400 fitted as master and Ikelite Substrobe 225 as slave. All film processing for this book, including the black and white photographs used to provide accurate reference material for Rico, was by Colab Ltd (Gladys Moore). Incidental machining and advice provided by Greenaway Marine of Swindon (Steve & Gerald Greenaway).

Research: Air Historical Branch RAF; Steve Cain; Nigel Cossons; Emperor Divers (Aaron Bruce, Louise Kraechter, Sarah Woodford); Fisher Nautical Books; David Fletcher; Chris Frost; Gilgeous Diving Services (Brian Gilgeous); Guildhall Library (various staff); Michael Hatlé; Illustrated London News Picture Library (Katie Simpson); Liverpool-Scottish Museum, (Ian Riley); Lloyd's Marine Archives; Lloyd's Register of Shipping (Emma Taaffe); Captain Dany Nakdimon; National Maritime Museum (Gabrielle Fabri, M. Sampson, Colin Starkey, R. G. Todd and numerous librarians); Newcastle-upon-Tyne Discovery Museum (Ian Whitehead); Steve Nichols; Kevin Patience; P & O Archives (Stephen Rabson); National Archives, Kew (Mark Dunton and various staff); RAF Hendon Museum (Peter Elliott); RAF Innsworth; Reederei Oldendorff (Bertram Sartoris); Royal Engineers Museum, Chatham (Craig Bowen); Royal Navy Museum, Portsmouth (Holly Downer, Allison Wareham); Scottish Maritime Museum (Jon Addison, Jim Grant, Mike Porter & Linda Ross); Seapics (Susan Dabritz); Shell Photographic Archives (Stephanie Versani); Simplon Postcards (Ian Boyle); Southampton City Library (Mark Illingworth, Penny Rudkin); South Tyneside Council Central Library (Doris Johnson); Tees Archaeology (Gary Green); Teesside Archives (Ann Thirsk); Tyne & Wear Archives Service (E. A. Rees); United Kingdom Hydrographic Office (June Dillon, Duncan Metcalfe, Glynis Furse, Peter Gange); Stefan Van Pellicom; Mark Webster and the World Ship Society (Tony Smith).

UK Tour Operators: Crusader Travel; Diving World; Eastern Sea Safaris (Brian & Barbara Evans and Hisham Abdel Azim); Pisces Diving (Pippa Oates); Red Sea Divers (David Easton) and Scubaway Travel (Neil Plowman).

Egyptian Diving Boats (Captains & Dive Guides): *Aziz 1* (Captain Bassem Mohammed Abu Ali and Paolo Guiotto); *Heba/Conquest II* (Captain Mohammed Said Hassan and John Watret); *Miss Nouran* (Captain Mohammed Hassan, Ali Baba and Geof Loe); *My Rosetta*

The propeller and rudder of the *Chrisoula K* may be large – but they are not as large as they appear in this photograph. This distortion occurred because Shane Brown was actually some distance away in the background.

(Captain Gafar Abrahim, Andi Dunkel, Vicki MacIntyre, Monika Hofbauer and David Giles); *Orchid* (Captain Sayed Moberk and Islam); *Pisces* (Captain Ahmed Farag and Mohammed); *Valerie* (Captain Abdul Aziz and Amro Shehata Eid Salem) and, finally, all their crews.

Airlines: Caledonian (Tom Lewis), Excel (Becky Steer), JMC, Monarch (Malcolm Tomlinson) and Sabre (Natalie).

Individuals: Tony Backhurst, John Bevan, Shane Brown, Adam Carruthers & Clair Cartwright (Hill Street Printers, Wisbech), Jon & Sam Dalton, Dr Carson Dron (Australia), Sue Eastment, Gaetano Franza, Andrew Goldby, Kimmo Hagman, Hans Hoffmann, Alan Holmes, Norman Hooke, Henk Joore (BSA Motorcycles), Roger Jordan, Michael Karger, Paul de Keijzer, Jarek Kowalski, Radhika Kumar, Richard Larn, Oliver Meisse, my son Daniel Middleton – for sorting out my computer equipment and my skills, Ian Morley, Peter Ormerod, Gary Parr, Osku Puukila, Howard Rosenstein, Grant Searancke, Dave Shields, Erkki Siirila, Alain Sobol, Peter Stollwerck, Bren Tierney, Andreas von Mach, Eric Watkins, Daniel Weaver and Ron Young.

Finally, a special mention for Lawson Wood. In an age where, generally speaking, people are not willing to help and assist someone who might be seen as a competitor, it was most refreshing to find a fellow professional underwater photo-journalist and author who was only too willing to help with many aspects of my research, and even provided some photographs. Let me know when I can return the favour...

◆ BIBLIOGRAPHY ◆

British Ocean Tramps Vol. 1 – Builders & Cargoes, P. N. Thomas, (Waine Research Publications, 1992), ISBN 0-905184-13-0

Conway's All the Worlds Fighting Ships 1922-1946, (Conway Maritime Press) ISBN 0-85177-146-7

Co159nway's All the Worlds Fighting Ships 1947-1995, (Conway Maritime Press), ISBN 0-85177-605-1

Dictionary of Disasters at Sea During the Age of Steam (1824–1962), Charles Hocking.

Dive to Adventure, Jack McKenney, (Gordon Soules, 1983), ISBN 0-919317-10-3

Diving the South – A mini-guide to the Southern Egyptian Red Sea, Ricard Buxó, (local publisher)

Encyclopaedia of Ships, The, (Orbis Publishing Ltd, 1995), ISBN 1-85605-288-5

Fifty Years of Naval Tugs, Bill Hannan, (Maritime Books), ISBN 0-907771-25-4

History of Ships, The, Peter Kemp, (Orbis, 1983), ISBN 0-84670-499-4

Hutchinson Factfinder Concise Encyclopaedia, E. M. Horsley, (Hutchinson, 1988)

Illustrated Marine Encyclopedia 1890, Captain H. Paasch, (facsimilie reprint, Argus 1977)

Jane's Fighting Ships of WW1, (Studio Editions, 1990), ISBN 1-85170-378-0

Jane's Fighting Ships of WW2, (Studio Editions, 1989), ISBN 1-85170-494-9

Maritime Casualties 1963-1996, Norman Hooke, ISBN 1-85978-110-1

Maritime History of the World Vol. 2, The, Duncan Haws & Alex A. Hurst, (Teredo Books, 1985), ISBN 0-90366-210-8

Modern Shipping Disasters 1963 – 1987 (Norman Hooke, 1989), ISBN 1-85044-211-8

Red Sea Pilot: Aden to Cyprus, Stephen Davis & Elaine Morgan, (Imray, Laurie, Norie & Wilson, 2002), ISBN 0-85288-554-7

Sharm el Sheikh Diving Guide (English Edition), Alberto Siliotti, ISBN 9-77304-000-3

Ships of the Royal Navy, J. J. Colledge, ISBN 0-94789-875-1

Thistle Boats, The, D. C. E. Burrell, (World Ship Society), ISBN 0-905617-43-6

Vital Guide to Fighting Aircraft of WW2, Edited by Karen Leverington, ISBN 1-85310-586-4

War Department Locomotives (R. Touret, 1976), ISBN 0-90587-800-0

World's Merchant Fleets 1939 (Roger Jordan, 1999), ISBN 1-86176-023-X

Wracktauchen – Die schönsten Wracks im Roten Meer, ISBN 3-79440-353-3 (Claus-Peter Stoll, Udo Kefrig & Christian Mietz)

Various volumes of *Lloyd's Register of Shipping* and *Lloyd's Lists*.

Numerous issues of House of Commons Parliamentary Papers, *Illustrated London News*, *National Geographic*, *Shipping & Mercantile Gazette*, *The Times* and the following scuba-diving magazines: *Diver*, *Scuba World*, *Sport Diver*, *Tauchen* and *Unterwasser*.

Sunsets in this part of the world can be quite spectacular.
One theory is that the red reflection of the setting sun on the sea is how the Red Sea came to be so named.